READINGS IN MODERN CHINESE LITERATURE

現代中國文學讀本

READINGS IN MODERN CHINESE LITERATURE

Volume One: Plays and Poems

YALE UNIVERSITY

NEW HAVEN, CONNECTICUT

Third Edition, 1968

by

Far Eastern Publications

First Edition, 1953

Second Edition, 1964

ISBN: 978-88710-071-0

TABLE OF CONTENTS

Notes

FOREWORD

Readings in Modern Chinese Literature is designed as a textbook for the student who, after two or three semesters of intensive study, has acquired a reading knowledge of colloquial Chinese and is ready to take up its literature. The book is divided into three volumes, covering (1) plays and poems, (2) stories and (3) essays of the last thirty five years from the beginning of the Literary Renaissance Movement in 1917 to the present time. It is by no means a representative anthology, but rather a collection of short, typical literary productions of the contemporary period. In making these selections, we have constantly kept in mind the interest of the materials, their suitability for classroom use, as well as the importance of the authors.

In the present volume, we have included four short plays and eleven poems. After finishing this volume, the student should be able to read longer and more difficult works as he goes further into the field of modern Chinese literature. To facilitate his understanding of the general background, against which these poems and plays were written, we have given here a brief introduction. The notes are intended to help students who use these volumes for classroom work or for outside reading.

In the preparation of this work, we have received help from many people, to whom we owe a debt of gratitude. We are particularly obliged to our fellow members of the Editorial Committee of the Institute of Far Eastern Languages, Yale University, for their constructive and profitable criticism.

Yale University   Tien-yi Li
New Haven, Conn.   Wu-chi Liu
March, 1953

INTRODUCTION

Modern Chinese drama is the product of the transitional age in which China found itself at the beginning of the twentieth century. During the past fifty years (1900 - 1950), the country has undergone cataclysmic changes embracing almost every aspect of Chinese life. The literary revolution of 1917, led by a group of university professors in Peking, marked the beginning of contemporary Chinese literature which stimulated a vigorous quickening of the intellectual pulses of the nation. By using literature as a powerful means of expression, many writers exercised great influence on contemporary Chinese thought.

As far as the drama is concerned, the new form is entirely different from the old. Modern Chinese theater has little in common with its predecessor, the Peking theater; even in language, there is a considerable dissimilarity between the two. Whereas the old drama was an operatic type with a great deal of poetry, singing, dancing, and gesticulating, the new drama is a spoken drama, or as the Chinese put it, *hua-chü* (hwàjyù) 話 劇 . Its dialogue is written in the everyday language of the people. In form, the new drama is divided into a number of acts and scenes and, like modern Western plays, has full stage directions. In content, it aims to represent the comedies and tragedies of real life. Sometimes, it also presents a message, an idea, or a social problem to engage the attention of its audience.

There are four stages in the evolution of this new drama. As early as the first years of the present century, a group of actors in Shanghai made an attempt to reform by introducing into the "New Theater" 新 舞 臺 they had built, realistic scenery and acting instead of the traditional Chinese use of symbols and simple stage property. But they confined their efforts to adapting old plays for modern presentation; as professional people, they were too much steeped in the conventions of the past to make any radical change. So it was not until 1912, the first year of the Chinese Republic, that a pioneering movement for the promotion of the new drama was set on foot. This was started by some Chinese students in Japan, who had formed there a dramatic organization called the Spring Willow Society 春 柳 社 , and who had experimented in playwriting and play production. When they returned to Shanghai, they produced some of the earliest Chinese plays in the spoken language. Among them, it will be interesting to note, were also adaptations of two Western stories, *La Dame aux Camélias* and *Uncle Tom's Cabin*. These, as well as the Chinese plays, were so successful on the stage that a vogue was created for this type of drama, which earned for itself the highly respectable name *Wen-ming Hsi* (Wénmíng Syì 文 明 戲), or "Civilized Play."

The success of the "Civilized Play," however, was only ephemeral; it soon declined and faded out. For one thing, its sponsors were all amateurs who had much zeal, but little time, for dramatics. The Spring Willow Society did not hold the stage long, nor did the other dramatic societies that mushroomed after it. In Shanghai, the theater was taken over by a group of business men, who were more interested in box office receipts than in dramatic art. They hired hack writers to do low comedies spiced with vulgar jokes, and melodramas with exciting stories geared to some ingenious mechanical device. The drama continued to be popular, but as a form of literary art it degenerated.

Then came the literary revolution that swept over the country like a thunderstorm. But its new ideas found little response in the traditional theatrical circle. The Peking drama, beautifully presented by Mei Lan-fang (Méi Lán-fāng) 梅 蘭 芳 , a famous female impersonator, was at best an art of the past; as for the "Civilized Play," it had become so vulgar that it was anything but what its name implied. Discouraged by the inadequacy of their dramatic heritage, the new writers turned to the West for guidance and set out on a new path of their own. Hu Shih (Hú Shì) 胡 適 , for instance, was one of the advocates for Western drama. In his essay on "Ibsenism", he expounded the modern view of drama as a realistic representation of life and as a vehicle for the propagation of ideas. An important dramatic theory had been formulated and presented to the Chinese public.

Chinese drama began to hold its own ground as a serious form of literature in the decade from 1917 to 1927. As early as 1921, the People's Dramatic Society 民 衆 戲 劇 社 was founded and the *Drama* 戲 劇 , the first Chinese periodical on drama, was published. This was followed in 1922 by the establishment of the first drama school in Peking, and in 1925 by the institution of a department of drama in the Peking Academy of Fine Arts 北 京 美 術 專 門 學 校 . Active in these movements were writers like Ou-yang Yü-ch'ien (Ōu-yáng Yú-chyàn) 歐 陽 予 倩 , a veteran member of the Spring Willow Society; Hsiung Fu-hsi (Syúng Fú-syī) 熊 佛 西 , head of the drama department in the Peking Academy of Fine Arts; T'ien Han (Tyán Hàn) 田 漢 , sponsor of the South China Society 南 國 社 , a literary association devoted to the dramatic arts; and Hung Shên (Húng Shēn) 洪 深 , an American-returned student who took the famous English 47 at Harvard under Professor G. P. Baker. All these men contributed to the development of the spoken drama by introducing the technique and practice of the West.

Also noteworthy because of its historical significance is Hu Shih's *Life's Great Affair* 終 身 大 事 , one of the earliest plays in the vernacular, dramatizing

· X ·

the story of a young woman who asserts her independence in matters of marriage by running away from her parents' home just as Nora in Ibsen's *A Doll's House* asserts her independence after marriage by leaving her husband's house.

Perhaps, the best play of this period is *Oppression* 壓 迫 by Ting Hsi-lin (Dīng Syī-lín) 丁 西 林, a physicist by profession and a dramatist by accident. His play is a sprightly comedy featuring an interesting house-hunting episode near Peking.

Among the other outstanding plays are *After Returning Home* 回 家 以 後 by Ou-yang Yü-ch'ien, a delightful comedy showing the dilemma of a returned student who had taken two wives; and *The Artist* 藝 術 家 by Hsiung Fu-hsi, a caricature of the attitude of society towards artists.

The next ten years, from 1927 to 1937, saw the rise of experimental theaters, school dramatics, and traveling companies of actors. By this time, the literary revolution had succeeded and the vernacular language was the chief literary medium of most writers. After years of constant application, the spoken words became more flexible and malleable, and hence well suited for use in the dialogue of a play. This proved to be a great asset to the new intellectuals, who were actively engaged in the creation of a modern Chinese literature. In drama, however, they still had many obstacles to conquer. They had to fight against not only the competition of the popular Peking theater, but also against the intrusion of American movies, which now held the stage in many big cities. Above all, the cost of producing plays was forbidding. It is true that some writers were willing to sacrifice their daily bread for the sake of art, but none of them had the resources to stage a play. In this dilemma, they were again encouraged by examples from abroad. Like the dramatic workers in England, Ireland, and elsewhere, they organized themselves into small groups, established little theaters, and experimented in playwriting and acting. They had the advantage of being in close contact with schools and colleges, in which were young men and women ardently dedicated to literature. In almost every school there was a dramatic club where students gave regular performances to train themselves in the theatrical art. It was in this kind of congenial atmosphere that Ts'ao Yü[1] (Tsáu Yú) 曹 禺, China's leading dramatist today, was nurtured and grew to maturity.

The literary career of Ts'ao Yü illustrates best the cross currents that were at work in the making of a modern Chinese playwright. These currents were, namely, the literary revolution of 1917, which set afire the imagination

---

1. Ts'ao Yü is the pen name of Wan Chia-pao (Wàn Jyā-bǎu) 萬 家 寶.

of young writers; the student movement of 1919, which awakened the intellectual class to its new responsibilities; the rising tide of literary activities in school; and the impact of Western thought upon the Chinese mind. All these influences are clearly discernible in the life and works of Ts'ao Yü. He was a member of a student dramatics club in high school, a graduate student majoring in Western literature, later a lecturer in the National Academy of Drama 國 立 戲 劇 學 校 in Chungking, and above all, a devoted dramatist.

Ts'ao Yü achieved fame with his first play *Thunder and Rain* 雷 雨 , which appeared in the *Literary Quarterly* 文 學 季 刊 in 1934 and was performed in the same year by a company of actors known as the Traveling Dramatic Troupe of China 中 國 旅 行 劇 團 . This group of actors toured many big cities such as Shanghai, Nanking, Tientsin, and Peking, where they presented *Thunder and Rain* as well as Chinese versions of Western plays such as *La Dame aux Camélias, Arms and the Man*, and *Lady Windermere's Fan.* But of all the plays in their repertoire, *Thunder and Rain*, which is a supreme drama of power and passion, was the most popular. The writers before Ts'ao Yü had produced clever farces and social comedies, but in *Thunder and Rain* as well as in his later plays like *Sunrise* 日 出 , *Wilderness* 原 野 , and *The Peking Man* 北 京 人 , Ts'ao Yü first mastered the art of tragedy. The appearance of his plays left little doubt that after years of apprenticeship and experiment, the Chinese had at last succeeded in producing a national drama of their own.

Encouraged by Ts'ao Yü's success, the dramatic world had just begun to be astir with life when its activities were suddenly disrupted by the Sino-Japanese War in 1937. At first this was disheartening. But, on the other hand, the war provided stimulus to the playwrights, and what is more important, extended the sphere of dramatic influence from urban to rural communities. The drama had already come to be a powerful weapon of propaganda and it is natural that it should now be employed to arouse nationalistic feelings among the masses. A new technique of playwriting, therefore, was evolved for performance at street corners, on village squares, and wherever a crowd gathered. These "street plays" were usually short pieces from one to three acts, simple enough to be enjoyed by rural and small-town audiences. The writers and actors were chiefly students and professionals who were encouraged by the government to participate in the war efforts.

During the war, the nation's cultural centers shifted from the coastal cities to the interior. In Chungking, the wartime capital, and Kweilin, a new literary stronghold, the theater continued to grow in spite of insurmountable difficulties. In fact, never before had Chinese drama been as prosperous as it was in the early days of the 1940's. There, in China's hinterland were gathered the literary talents of the country, who individually or in collaboration produced some of the best plays in the vernacular language. A host of new writers joined the old, and together they made the drama the most important literary contribution to the war. Older dramatists like Ou-yang Yü-ch'ien, T'ien Han, and Hung Shên were active in composing propaganda plays, in organizing and directing dramatic troupes, and in touring the countryside with their productions. To the war effort Ts'ao Yü added the play *Metamorphosis* 蛻 變, in which the bravery, perseverance, and self-sacrifice of a female doctor in a war hospital are exalted. A play with a somewhat similar theme is the *Tale of a Frontier City* 邊 城 故 事 which dramatizes the heroic effort of the director of a government-owned gold mine. Its author, Yüan Chün[2] (Ywán Jyùn) 袁 俊, an American-returned student trained at the Drama School in Yale, also wrote the famous play, *Model Teacher of a Myriad Generations* 萬 世 師 表, about a college professor who carries on his teaching and research in the midst of personal privation. In *The Fascist Bacillus* 法 西 斯 細 菌 by Hsia Yen[3] (Syà Yěn) 夏 衍, a bacteriologist is the hero. All these characters are taken from life and their patriotism is idealized as an example for the people. On the other hand, the dramatists presented villains such as spies and traitors in enemy-occupied Shanghai and corrupt officials and greedy merchants in war-torn Chungking. Such people were attacked in plays like *The Dance of the Devils* 羣 魔 亂 舞 and *Misty Chungking* 霧 重 慶, written respectively by Ch'ên Pai-ch'ên (Chén Bái-chén) 陳 白 塵 and Sung Chih-ti (Sùng Jř-dì) 宋 之 的, both well known for their productivity during the war.

Not all the plays, however, deal with war. *The Spring and Autumn of Drama* 戲 劇 春 秋, a collaboration of Sung Chih-ti and two other writers, is a resumé of the dramatic activities of modern China. *The Cowherd Boy and the Weaving Maid* 牛 郎 織 女 by Wu Tsu-kuang (Wú Dzǔ-gwāng) 吳 祖 光 revives the beautiful Chinese legend of two fairy lovers who can meet only once a year across the Milky Way. Historical plays too were popular. Kuo Mo-jo (Gwō Mwò-rwò) 郭 沫 若, a veteran writer and critic in the early days of the literary revolution, returned to the theater with a number of histories, including one of Ch'ü Yüan (Chyū Ywán) 屈 原, a patriotic poet and statesman of ancient China, in whose honor the Dragon Boat Festival was held. Yang Ts'un-pin (Yáng Tswūn-bīn) 楊 村 彬, a professor at the National Academy of Drama in Chungking, became famous for his trilogy *The Unofficial History of the Ch'ing Palace* 清 宮 外 史, in which historical figures

2. Yüan Chün is the pen name of Chang Chün-hsiang (Jāng Jyùn-syáng) 張 駿 祥

3. Hsia Yen is the pen name of Shen Tuan-hsien (Shěn Dwān-syān) 沈 端 先.

like the Empress Dowager Tz'u-hsi (Tsźsyī) 慈 禧 , the Kuang-hsü (Gwāng-syù) 光 緒 Emperor, Li Hung-chang (Lǐ Húng-jāng) 李 鴻 章 , and Yüan Shih-k'ai (Ywán Shǐ-kǎi) 袁 世 凱 came alive on the stage. There is little doubt that these successes placed the historical play on a par with the social comedy, family tragedy, and war play as a major division of contemporary Chinese drama.

After the end of the Sino-Japanese War in 1945, Shanghai regained its leading position in the dramatic world. A number of new plays were produced there, and hopes for a period of prosperity ran high. But in 1948, the theatrical business was again interrupted by war, this time an internecine one, which resulted in the introduction of a new form of government, a new social system, a new ideology for the Chinese people, and a new direction in literature. Thus, to summarize the dramatic achievements of the contemporary period, it may be said that though there will be new emphasis and changes in content, the fundamental technique and craftsmanship of modern playwriting, which the Chinese took all these years to learn, will not have been learned in vain. It is equally certain, that Chinese drama will continue to reflect life as it is and Chinese dramatists will continue to write, whenever circumstances are favorable, with renewed vim and increasing maturity.

Modern Chinese poetry, like the drama, owed its existence to the literary revolution of 1917. One of the burning issues at that time was whether a new form of poetry should be evolved to replace the conventional form. In the course of China's long literary history, few writers left specimens of poetry that broke completely away from the traditions of the past. Having grown up under the shadow of their great ancestors, Chinese poets today find it hard to deviate from time-honored methods and techniques. On the one hand, it is difficult for the new writers to excel in the art which their predecessors long ago brought to perfection. On the other hand, this art has been pampered, its forms have become stereotyped, and the possibilities and resources of the language have been so exhausted that modern writers cannot hope to contribute anything original and worthwhile unless they create a new form and rhythm of their own. This is just what the poets of modern China have attempted to do.

In order to achieve this aim, they have introduced a revolutionary change in poetic style by using the *pai-hua* (báihwà) 白 話 or the colloquial language. This innovation was contrary to Chinese literary tradition and ran into great opposition at the very outset. It is true that some early Chinese poets did advocate the use of a simple diction in poetry, but it was inconceivable that anyone should write poems in the words of everyday conversation. Therefore, during the first years of the literary revolution, the orthodox critics were particularly vehement in their denunciation of the new poets who used "the language of the street-hawkers and cart-pullers".

In this battle of languages, the champion of the vernacular was Hu Shih, who had just returned from America and was freshly equipped with the ideas and ideals of the West. Brushing aside the criticism of the opposition, he urged his fellow writers to free themselves from the shackles of the past and start out on a path of their own. Not content to be a mere theorist, he put his theory into practice by publishing the first vernacular poem in the *New Youth Magazine* 新青年 of January, 1918. This was followed a year later by his essay "A Discourse on New Poetry" 談新詩 and in March, 1920, by his first volume of vernacular poetry, fittingly entitled *Experimental Poems* 嘗試集.

The pioneering work of Hu Shih was immediately hailed by a number of writers and produced a wave of poetic activities throughout the country. In the decade following the publication of the *Experimental Poems*, many other volumes of poetry, some rather immature, poured forth from the press, and by dint of their sheer weight and bulk, managed to crush the opposition of their critics. By 1930, the *pai-hua* poets had become firmly established in the world of letters, which they shared with the novelists, essayists, and playwrights of the time. Wielded by them with ease and dexterity, the vernacular became the accepted medium of poetry. With this change in language came a corresponding change in style, form, and content. Shapeless as most of the new verses were, they expressed likewise the poet's feelings without restraint. The scope of poetry, too, was broadened to include any subject. It might be the heart-rending wail of a poetic soul in agony, the battle cries of a hot-eyed young revolutionary, the bitter protests of an oppressed factory worker, or the happy exaltations of a sentimentalist deeply awed by the grandeur of nature.

During these years of experimentation, three schools of poetry emerged. The first consisted of a group of poets who were students and teachers in the universities in Peking. Like Hu Shih, they were academicians who strove to free themselves from the conventions of classical poetry, in which they were reared, only to find that their revolt was half-hearted, and their success, partial. To be sure, they wrote in the spoken language, and their poems are *vers libres* without rhyme and meter. But they were so bound by the great tradition that they could hardly erase the vestiges of the past. The earmarks of the old poetry, particularly its diction, remained. Moreover, what made their poems truly experimental, or rather eclectic, was that they borrowed both ideas and modes of expression from Western poetry so that in their verses there was a curious blending of East and West. Outstanding among them were Liu Fu (Lyóu Fù) 劉復 , a contributor to the *New Youth* and a promotor of the vernacular language, and Ping Hsin[4] (Bīng Syīn) 冰心 , whose lyrics have a touch that is tender and exquisitely feminine. As a whole, most of these experimenters left volumes of poems remembered for their historical significance rather than for their intrinsic value.

Another group of writers, most of them returned students from Japan, combined forces under the banner of the Creative Society 創造社 which had its headquarters in Shanghai. They published periodicals and individual works that had a wide influence in the early days of the new literary movement. The boundless activities of these men is typified by Kuo Mo-jo, who wrote voluminously in every kind of literature. His poems form a school by themselves. They represent the impassioned utterances of a restless soul which disdains to be curbed by restraint. Instead of recollecting his emotions in tranquility, he gave such free rein to his overflowing sentiments that they seem to inundate the dikes of reason and become a torrential deluge. A sentimentalist, he introduced into his poems exclamations, slogans, and loud protestations that disarm his reader by the heat of his passion. As a revolutionary, he attacked not only the conventional ways of writing, but also the conventions of society itself. In this way, he considerably expanded the scope of Chinese poetry and made it a powerful means of propaganda.

Opposed to the Creative Society was the Crescent Society 新月社 , founded by a number of returned students from America. Due to their training in classical Western literature, they regarded form as an essential part of poetry. In the famous words of their theorist, Wên I-to (Wén Yī-dwō) 聞一多 , they delighted in "dancing in fetters." These fetters, however, were not all made in China, some of them being imported from abroad. Their belief was that emotions can be best expressed in regulated meters which help to keep the poet's fancy from running riot. Since Chinese poetic forms are too few and limited, it is necessary to create new verses with a definite rhyme and rhythm; therefore, nothing could be more handy than to borrow from the existing forms of Western poetry. A good example is the sonnet, used by the Crescent poets as a trumpet to blow their "soul-animating strains."

Foremost among the poets of this school was Hsü Chih-mo (Syú Jǐ-mwó) 徐志摩 , whose poetic career was cut short in an airplane accident. Like his fellow Crescenters, Hsü Chih-mo was devoted to poetry. His verses show

---

4. Ping Hsin is the pen name of Hsien Wan-ying (Syè Wǎn-yíng) 謝婉瑩

signs of the gradual maturing of vernacular poetry from an experimental to a creative stage. His poems are characterized by a delicacy, an aesthetic joy, a true feeling for words as well as an awareness of the importance of form. This awareness was shared by Wên I-to, poet, painter, and scholar. In his last years, he took part in political activities that resulted in his assassination. Besides two volumes of poems, Wên I-to contributed many literary and political essays which greatly influenced the minds of the younger generation, of whom he was as indefatigable teacher. In contrast to Wen's varied interests, the life-long passion of Chu Hsiang (Jū Syāng) 朱 湘 was verse writing. He was a poet, pure and simple. Neglecting all practical considerations, he lived in poetry and he dreamed of poetry. In fact he was so absorbed in his ethereal flights that when he found them incompatible with the sordidness of his surroundings, he gave up life by drowning himself in the Yangtze. It is sad to note that an untimely end came to each one of the three Crescent poets, thus preventing them from attaining the fulness of their poetic brilliancy.

But stimulated by their persistent efforts, modern Chinese poetry made good headway in the mid—1930's. One of the important events in those years was the publication of the *New Poetic Treasury* 新 詩 庫 in ten volumes. It contains the writings of a number of young poets who came under Hsü Chih-mo's influence. In the same *Treasury*, however, were also the works of others who represented a new symbolic trend in poetry. Imagism, as it had appeared earlier in the poems of Li Chin-fa (Lǐ Jīn-fǎ) 李 金 髮 and Tai Wang-shu (Dài Wàng-shū) 戴 望 舒 , both trained in France, became the fashion of the day. Tai Wang-shu, especially, wrote many poems and poetic critiques, and edited a magazine of verse called *New Poetry* 新 詩 . According to him, the rhythm of poetry depends not so much upon the cadence of music as upon that of the emotions, which cannot be regulated by any rhyme or meter. For illustration, he and others translated French poets like Paul Verlaine, Jules Laforgue, and Paul Valéry to serve as models for the fledgling Chinese imagists.

In the same period there appeared a slender but remarkable volume of poetry by three friends, Li Kuang-t'ien (Lǐ Gwǎng-tyán) 李 廣 田 , Pien Chih-lin (Byàn Jř-lín) 卞 之 琳 , and Ho Ch'i-fang (Hé Chí-fāng) 何 其 芳 . *The Garden of Han* 漢 園 集 , taken from the name of a street in Peking, is an important landmark in contemporary Chinese poetry. It is a joint enterprise of three former schoolmates in the National University of Peking 國 立 北 京 大 學 or Peita (Běidà) 北 大 . They were about the same age, lived together in the same quarters, and were moved, no doubt, by the same inspiration. Both Li Kuang-t'ien and Pien Chih-lin majored in European literature, while Ho Ch'i-fang, a student of philosophy, also loved poetry. Though different in their personal traits and capabilities—Li Kuang-t'ien with his peasant strain and a longing for the soil, Pien Chih-lin with his translations from Baudelaire and Mallarmé, and Ho Ch'i-fang with his classical education—in the *Garden of Han* they showed the same subtlety of feeling, the same dexterity in the use of the colloquial language, and the same sensitivity to the rhythm of poetry. Above all, they had a common intellectual approach to their subjects, whether these were imaginary or realistic.

The Peita trio were joined by several other poets of talent. Among them were Fêng Chih (Féng Jr̀) 馮 至 , author of sonnets; Tsang K'o-chia (Dzāng Kè-jyā) 臧 克 家, known for his *Self-Portrait* 自 己 的 寫 照 , a long autobiographical poem of one thousand lines; and Ai Ch'ing (Ài Chīng) 艾 青 , whose *Ta-yen* (Dàyàn) *River* 大 堰 河 contains a moving story of the struggles and sufferings of the author's wet nurse. It is a sustained narrative poem told in racy and vigorous words that leave an unforgettable impression on the reader. It is no wonder that the *Ta-yen River*, the title also of a collection of his poems, won immediate nationwide acclaim, and made Ai Ch'ing the most famous of the modern poets.

The works of all these poets were published before the Sino-Japanese War in 1937. As might be expected, the war changed Chinese poetry, as it did the novel and the drama, into a more articulate and virile form of literature with a wider appeal to the masses. Like others, the poets heeded the patriotic call and went to the front to record and sing the heroic deeds of the soldiers. At that time, China's vast and limitless Northwest became for many writers the symbol of resistance. Even a novelist like Lao Shê[5] (Lǎu Shě) 老 舍 would visit these regions and come back with a ten-thousand line poem on his expedition there. Others like Pien Chih-lin and Ho Ch'i-fang went to live with the peasant partisans and learned firsthand of the war life which they described in their writings. Still others like Ai Ch'ing stayed in the north and wrote of the people of the "Northern Land" 北 方 as well as "The Man Who Died a Second Death" 他 死 在 第 二 次 , a war poem exalting the bravery and patriotism of the common soldier. There were also poets who fought and fell in the war. A notable example is P'u Feng (Pú Fēng) 蒲 風 , a well-known author, who joined the army of resistance in South China and was killed in action at the age of twenty-eight. Besides, there were poets among the guerrilla fighters, but very little of their writings was circulated outside the war area.

Last of all, mention should be made of T'ien Chien[6] (Tyán Jȳan) 田 間 ,

5. Lao Shê is the pen name of Shu Shê-yü (Shū Shê-yú) 舒 舍 予 .

6. T'ien Chien is the pen name of T'ung T'ien-chien (Túng Tyān-jyán) 童 天 鑑 .

who became popular for his short, rugged, sinewy verses that defy all known rules of versification. To a certain extent, T'ien Chien's poems recall the exclamatory lines of Kuo Mo-jo, but T'ien Chien possesses a directness and vigor that are not found in the elder poet. Moreover, T'ien Chien's themes are by no means romantic or sentimental; instead, they are realistic and down-to-earth. They smell of the soil and the gunpowder; they sound the battle cry of modern times. His is a revolutionary poetry par excellence; a poetry with emotions that run amok and outcries that are deafening and nerve-wracking. Indeed, T'ien Chien might be called a "drummer of his age" for his attempts to arouse it from spiritual lethargy, but his persistent tom-toms are not likely to become a major voice in the symphony of poetry.

To sum up the progress of contemporary verse, Chinese poetry is not as great as it should be in a land of great poetry. Its growth seems to have been rather slow and uncertain. But it is good to know that the soil has been tilled, the weeds have been cleared, and the seeds sown; the sprouts too are coming up.

COMPARATIVE TRANSCRIPTION TABLE

Yale Wade-Giles Pinyin

Yale	Wade-Giles	Pinyin	Yale	Wade-Giles	Pinyin
a	a	a	chye	ch'ieh	qie
ai	ai	ai	chyou	ch'iu	qiu
an	an	an	chyu	ch'ü	qu
ang	ang	ang	chyun	ch'ün	qun
au	ao	ao	chyung	ch'iung	qiong
			chywan	ch'üan	quan
ba	pa	ba	chywe	ch'üeh	que
bai	pai	bai			
ban	pan	ban	da	ta	da
bang	pang	bang	dai	tai	dai
bau	pao	bao	dan	tan	dan
bei	pei	bei	dang	tang	dang
ben	pen	ben	dau	tao	dao
beng	peng	beng	de	te	de
bi	pi	bi	dei	tei	dei
bin	pin	bin	deng	teng	deng
bing	ping	bing	di	ti	di
bou	pou	bou	ding	ting	ding
bu	pu	bu	dou	tou	dou
bwo	po	bo	du	tu	du
byan	pien	bian	dung	tung	dong
byau	piao	biao	dwan	tuan	duan
bye	pieh	bie	dwei	tui	dui
			dwo	to	duo
cha	ch'a	cha	dwun	tun	dun
chai	ch'ai	chai	dyan	tien	dian
chan	ch'an	chan	dyau	tiao	diao
chang	ch'ang	chang	dye	tieh	die
chau	ch'ao	chao	dyou	tiu	diu
che	ch'e	che	dz	tzu	zi
chen	ch'en	chen	dza	tsa	za
cheng	ch'eng	cheng	dzai	tsai	zai
chi	ch'i	qi	dzan	tsan	zan
chin	ch'in	qin	dzang	tsang	zang
ching	ch'ing	qing	dzau	tsao	zao
chou	ch'ou	chou	dze	tse	ze
chr	ch'ih	chi	dzei	tsei	zei
chu	ch'u	chu	dzen	tsen	zen
chung	ch'ung	chong	dzeng	tseng	zeng
chwai	ch'uai	chuai	dzou	tsou	zou
chwan	ch'uan	chuan	dzu	tsu	zu
chwang	ch'uang	chuang	dzung	tsung	zong
chwei	ch'ui	chui	dzwan	tsuan	zuan
chwo	ch'o	chuo	dzwei	tsui	zui
chwun	ch'un	chun	dzwo	tso	zuo
chya	ch'ia	qia	dzwun	tsun	zun
chyan	ch'ien	qian			
chyang	ch'iang	qiang	e	e, o	e
chyau	ch'iao	qiao	ei	ei	ei

Yale	Wade-Giles	Pinyin	Yale	Wade-Giles	Pinyin
en	en	en	jau	chao	zhao
eng	eng	eng	je	che	zhe
er	erh	er	jei	chei	zhei
			jen	chen	zhen
fa	fa	fa	jeng	cheng	zheng
fan	fan	fan	ji	chi	ji
fang	fang	fang	jin	chin	jin
fei	fei	fei	jing	ching	jing
fen	fen	fen	jou	chou	zhou
feng	feng	feng	jr	chih	'zhi
fou	fou	fou	ju	chu	zhu
fu	fu	fu	jung	chung	zhong
fwo	fo	fo	jwa	chua	zhua
			jwai	chuai	zhuai
ga	ka	ga	jwan	chuan	zhuan
gai	kai	gai	jwang	chuang	zhuang
gan	kan	gan	jwei	chui	zhui
gang	kang	gang	jwo	cho	zhuo
gau	kao	gao	jwun	chun	zhun
ge	ke, ko	ge	jya	chia	jia
gei	kei	gei	jyan	chien	jian
gen	ken	gen	jyang	chiang	jiang
geng	keng	geng	jyau	chiao	jiao
gou	kou	gou	jye	chieh	jie
gu	ku	gu	jyou	chiu	jiu
gung	kung	gong	jyu	chü	ju
gwa	kua	gua	jyun	chün	jun
gwai	kuai	guai	jyung	chiung	jiong
gwan	kuan	guan	jywan	chüan	juan
gwang	kuang	guang	jywe	chüeh	jue
gwei	kuei	gui			
gwo	kuo	guo	ka	k'a	ka
gwun	kun	gun	kai	k'ai	kai
			kan	k'an	kan
ha	ha	ha	kang	k'ang	kang
hai	hai	hai	kau	k'ao	kao
han	han	han	ke	k'e, k'o	ke
hang	hang	hang	ken	k'en	ken
hau	hao	hao	keng	k'eng	keng
he	ho	he	kou	k'ou	kou
hei	hei	hei	ku	k'u	ku
hen	hen	hen	kung	k'ung	kong
heng	heng	heng	kwa	k'ua	kua
hou	hou	hou	kwai	k'uai	kuai
hu	hu	hu	kwan	k'uan	kuan
hung	hung	hong	kwang	k'uang	kuang
hwa	hua	hua	kwei	k'uei	kui
hwai	huai	huai	kwo	k'uo	kuo
hwan	huan	huan	kwun	k'un	kun
hwang	huang	huang			
hwei	hui	hui	la	la	la
hwo	huo	huo	lai	lai	lai
hwun	hun	hun	lan	lan	lan
			lang	lang	lang
ja	cha	zha	lau	lao	lao
jai	chai	zhai	le	le	le
jan	chan	zhan	lei	lei	lei
jang	chang	zhang	leng	leng	leng

Yale	Wade-Giles	Pinyin	Yale	Wade-Giles	Pinyin
li	li	li	nyau	niao	niao
lin	lin	lin	nye	nieh	nie
ling	ling	ling	nyou	niu	niu
lou	lou	lou	nyu	nü	nü
lu	lu	lu	nywe	nüeh	nüe
lung	lung	long			
lwan	luan	luan	ou	ou	ou
lwo	lo	luo			
lwun	lun	lun	pa	p'a	pa
lya	lia	lia	pai	p'ai	pai
lyan	lien	lian	pan	p'an	pan
lyang	liang	liang	pang	p'ang	pang
lyau	liao	liao	pau	p'ao	pao
lye	lieh	lie	pei	p'ei	pei
lyou	liu	liu	pen	p'en	pen
lyu	lü	lü	peng	p'eng	peng
lywan	lüan	lüan	pi	p'i	pi
lywe	lüeh	lüe	pin	p'in	pin
			ping	p'ing	ping
ma	ma	ma	pou	p'ou	pou
mai	mai	mai	pu	p'u	pu
man	man	man	pwo	p'o	po
mang	mang	mang	pyan	p'ien	pian
mau	mao	mao	pyau	p'iao	piao
mei	mei	mei	pye	p'ieh	pie
men	men	men			
meng	meng	meng	r	jih	ri
mi	mi	mi	ran	jan	ran
min	min	min	rang	jang	rang
ming	ming	ming	rau	jao	rao
mou	mou	mou	re	je	re
mu	mu	mu	ren	jen	ren
mwo	mo	mo	reng	jeng	reng
myan	mien	mian	rou	jou	rou
myau	miao	miao	ru	ju	ru
mye	mieh	mie	rung	jung	rong
myou	miu	miu	rwan	juan	ruan
			rwei	jui	rui
na	na	na	rwo	jo	ruo
nai	nai	nai	rwun	jun	run
nan	nan	nan			
nang	nang	nang	sa	sa	sa
nau	nao	nao	sai	sai	sai
ne	ne	ne	san	san	san
nei	nei	nei	sang	sang	sang
nen	nen	nen	sau	sao	sao
neng	neng	neng	se	se	se
ni	ni	ni	sen	sen	sen
nin	nin	nin	seng	seng	seng
ning	ning	ning	sha	sha	sha
nou	nou	nou	shai	shai	shai
nu	nu	nu	shan	shan	shan
nung	nung	nong	shang	shang	shang
nwan	nuan	nuan	shau	shao	shao
nwo	no	nuo	she	she	she
nwun	nun	nun	shei	shei	shei
nyan	nien	nian	shen	shen	shen
nyang	niang	niang	sheng	sheng	sheng

Yale	Wade-Giles	Pinyin	Yale	Wade-Giles	Pinyin
shou	shou	shou	tsau	ts'ao	cao
shr	shih	shi	tse	ts'e	ce
shu	shu	shu	tsen	ts'en	cen
shwa	shua	shua	tseng	ts'eng	ceng
shwai	shuai	shuai	tsou	ts'ou	cou
shwan	shuan	shuan	tsu	ts'u	cu
shwang	shuang	shuang	tsung	ts'ung	cong
shwei	shui	shui	tswan	ts'uan	cuan
shwo	shuo	shuo	tswei	ts'ui	cui
shwun	shun	shun	tswo	ts'o	cuo
sou	sou	sou	tswun	ts'un	cun
su	su	su	tsz	tz'u	ci
sung	sung	song	tu	t'u	tu
swan	suan	suan	tung	t'ung	tong
swei	sui	sui	twan	t'uan	tuan
swo	so	suo	twei	t'ui	tui
swun	sun	sun	two	t'o	tuo
sya	hsia	xia	twun	t'un	tun
syan	hsien	xian	tyan	t'ien	tian
syang	hsiang	xiang	tyau	t'iao	tiao
syau	hsiao	xiao	tye	t'ieh	tie
sye	hsieh	xie			
syi	hsi	xi	wa	wa	wa
syin	hsin	xin	wai	wai	wai
sying	hsing	xing	wan	wan	wan
syou	hsiu	xiu	wang	wang	wang
syu	hsü	xu	wei	wei	wei
syun	hsün	xun	wen	wen	wen
syung	hsiung	xiong	weng	weng	weng
sywan	hsüan	xuan	wo	wo	wo
sywe	hsüeh	xue	wu	wu	wu
sz	ssu, szu	si			
			ya	ya	ya
ta	t'a	ta	yai	yai	yai
tai	t'ai	tai	yan	yen	yan
tan	t'an	tan	yang	yang	yang
tang	t'ang	tang	yau	yao	yao
tau	t'ao	tao	ye	yeh	ye
te	t'e	te	yi	yi, i	yi
teng	t'eng	teng	yin	yin	yin
ti	t'i	ti	ying	ying	ying
ting	t'ing	ting	you	yu	you
tou	t'ou	tou	yu	yü	yu
tsa	ts'a	ca	yun	yün	yun
tsai	ts'ai	cai	yung	yung	yong
tsan	ts'an	can	ywan	yüan	yuan
tsang	ts'ang	cang	ywe	yüeh	yue

NOTES

Volume one: Plays and Poems

Prepared by

Wu-chi Liu, Tien-yi Li, and Grace Wan

壓　迫　*Yāpwò*

丁西林　　*Dīng Syī-lín* （1893 - ） Playwright and scientist. Born in Taihsing, Kiangsu. He completed his advanced education in England and after his return to China, taught physics in the universities in Peking. From 1928 to 1945 he was director of the Institute of Physics, Academia Sinica. He was one of the Chinese delegates who visited India in 1951 on a good-will tour sponsored by the Communist government in Peking.

Though an amateur dramatist, he has contributed a number of one-act plays which are well-made and intensely popular. Recently some of his short plays have been revived and staged by Chinese students in New York.

page 3

	壓迫	*yāpwò* oppression ; to oppress
5	老媽子	*lāumādz* maidservant
6	巡警	*syúnjīng* policeman
8	耳房	*ěrfáng* side room
	偏	*pyān* to incline towards
9	煤油燈	*mèiyóu dēng* kerosene lamp
	茶具	*chájyù* tea service such as cups, pot and tray
10	茶几	*chájī* a small side table
11	手提的皮包	*shōutide píbāu* handbag
	類似	*lèisż* somewhat like

page 4

1	花瓶	*hwā píng* flower vase
	陳設	*chénshè* arrangement, furnishing
	儉樸	*jyǎnpǔ* to be plain, simple, frugal
2	著	*jwo* to wear

NOTES

	粗呢	*tsū ni* coarse wool
	長筒皮靴	*chángtǔng pí sywē* long-legged boots
2	煙斗	*yāndǒu* pipe
3	簷	*yán* eaves
4	代	*dài* for (used like 給)
6	不耐煩	*búnàifán* to be impatient (lit., cannot bear the boredom)
9	嘆氣	*tànchì* to sigh (嘆了一口氣 heaved a sigh)
10	橫豎	*héngshù* in any case, anyway (lit., horizontal or vertical)
11	復	*fù* again
13	定錢	*dìngchyan* deposit (money)
14	脾氣	*píchi* temper
	古怪	*gǔgwài* to be odd, queer
15	有甚麼要緊	*yǒu shémma yaùjǐn* what does it matter; there is nothing to worry about
	深更半夜	*shēn gēng bàn yè* late at night; during midnight (更 means night-watch. Every two hours the watchman makes his rounds.)
	照應	*jàuying* to look after, care for

page 5

2	並	*bíng* indeed (intensive particle before a negative)
3	顯亮	*syǔnlyàng* to be open and bright
6	外人	*wàiren* outsider, stranger (Cf., P. 94, L. 5)
	打牌	*dǔpái* to play mahjong, cards, etc.
8	家眷	*jyājywan* family, wife and children
9	回了	*hwéile* sent away

| 12 | 吵 | *cȟau* to quarrel |
| | 做主 | *dzwòjǔ* to make a decision; to take the responsibility (lit., to act as a master) (same as 作主) |

page 6

2	砰	*pèng* to meet; to run against (砰在一塊兒 to come or bump together)
4	嘈雜	*tsáudzá* to be noisy and confused
11	犯罪	*fándzwèi* to commit crime
13	瞎想	*syā syǔng* to think rashly or foolishly
14	少停	*shǔu tíng* after a short pause, a little while
16	勞	*láu* to trouble

page 7

1	打攪	*dǎjyǎu* to trouble; to put one to inconvenience
2	皮夾子	*píjyādz* wallet
	票子	*pyàudz* dollar-bill, bank-note
10	不快	*búkwài* to be displeased
11	由	*yóu* by, from
13	退	***twèi*** to give up, withdraw, retreat

page 8

3	廢話	*fèihwà* useless talk
5	毫無	*háu wú* absolutely not (毫 is an intensifier used before a negative like 無 and 不.)
10	爭論	*jēnglwùn* to argue
11	和事老	*héshr̀ lǔu* peace-maker
12	宵	*syāu* night

NOTES

13   固執   *gùjr*   to be stubborn

page 9

11   煙包   *yānbāu*   tobacco pouch

      煙罐   *yāngwàn*   can of tobacco

13   敲   *chyāu*   to strike, knock

      厲聲   *lì shēng*   in a harsh voice

      仍然   *réngrán*   still, as before

15   勢子   *shìrdz*   gesture, manner, appearance

      原諒   *ywánlyàng*   to forgive

page 10

1   一連   *yīlyán*   successively, continuously

3   氣還未平   *chī hái wèi ping*   (his) anger has not yet subsided, not yet calmed down

      啣   *syán*   to hold in the mouth

8   對頭   *dwèitou*   opponent

10   狠心   *hěnsyīn*   relentlessly, fiercely

12   打濕   *dǎshī*   to get wet

      發酸   *fāswān*   to become sore (lit., sour)

15   觀察   *gwānchá*   to observe, examine

16   引起   *yǐnchǐ*   to arouse

      趣味   *chyùwei*   interest

page 11

1   担任   *dānrèn*   to take up; to bear the responsibility

2   登廣告   *dēnggwǎnggàu*   to publish an advertisement

• 8–11 •

3	聘請	*pìngchǐng* to engage, employ
	書記	*shūjì* secretary
5	啓事	*chǐshr̀* announcement, notice
	敝公司	*bì gūngsz̄* our company (敝 low, unworthy, or humble, is a polite term for first person singular or plural in expressions such as 敝人 or 鄙人, I myself; 敝姓 my name, etc.)
6	親友	*chīnyǒu* relatives and friends
	薦書	*jyànshū* letter of recommendation (薦 is also written as 荐.)
	恕	*shù* please excuse, forgive
	作覆	*dzwòfù* to reply
	特此聲明	*tè tsž shēng míng* this is specially announced (a common expression used in the concluding part of a public notice)
10	得意	*déyì* to be pleased, elated
11	瞞	*mán* to conceal (不瞞你說 I'll not conceal it from you; to tell you the truth)

page 12

2	紙煙盒	*jǐryān hé* cigarette case
7	不僅	*bújǐn* not only
8	殷勤	*yīnchin* to be attentive and obliging
12	幹麼	*gànmá* for what, why (same as 爲什麼)
13	漆黑	*chīhēi* to be pitch-dark
15	如有所思	*rú yǒu swǒ sz̄* as if thinking of some thing; contemplating
16	告辭	*gàutsź* to take leave, say good-bye

page 13

2	阻止	*dzǔjř* to prevent, stop

NOTES

12 不然　　　*bùrán* otherwise

　　説話　　　*hwǔnghwà* a lie

page 14

2 閙鬼　　　*nàugwěi* to be haunted by ghosts

6 蘆葦　　　*lúwěi* reed, mat, straw

7 頂篷　　　*dǐngpéng* ceiling

　　洋灰　　　*yánghwēi* cement (lit., foreign lime)

　　現成　　　*syànchéng* to be ready-made, furnished

　　舖蓋　　　*pūgai* beddings

8 撩　　　　*lyáu* to pull up

12 再…沒有了　*dzài . . . méiyǒu le* could not be more . . .

page 15

4 挺　　　　*tǐng* to straighten up

　　胸脯　　　*syūngpǔ* chest (脯 is flesh of the chest)

　　豎起　　　*shùchi* to raise; to lift up

　　眉毛　　　*méimau* eyebrow

5 補　　　　*bǔ* to add, supplement (here, to repeat)

8 侮辱　　　*wǔrù* insult

11 干　　　　*gān* to concern (干你甚麼事 what has that to do with you? that's none of your business)

15 性急　　　*syìng jí* to be impatient, quick-tempered

page 16

6 工程師　　*gūngchéngshř* engineer

10 搶着説　　*chyǎngje shwō* to interrupt (搶 to snatch)

page 17

5 　盤問 　　*pánwèn*　to cross-examine

11　要挾 　　*yāusyé*　to make unreasonable and threatenting demand, to coerce

　　可惡 　　*kèwù*　to be hateful, disgusting, or wicked

page 18

1 　教訓 　　*jyàusyun*　to instruct （教訓了一頓 gave a lecture; reprimanded）

10　攆 　　　*nyān*　to throw out

13　怪有趣 　*gwài youchyù*　to be quite interesting, funny or amusing

16　痛打 　　*tùng dǎ*　to beat soundly

page 19

4 　出那口氣 *chū nèikǒu chì*　to vent one's anger, to have revenge

6 　少頓 　　*shǎu dwùn*　a short pause

8 　求婚 　　*chyóuhwūn*　to propose marriage

9 　誤會 　　*wùhwei*　to misunderstand

10　妙 　　　*myàu*　to be clever, wonderful or excellent

13　損害 　　*swǔnhài*　harm

page 20

3 　嗤 　　　*chī*　an interjection to signify scoff

　　側耳 　　*tsèěr*　to cock an ear, to incline the ear

6 　急促 　　*jítsù*　hastily

8 　吵了嘴 　*chǎule dzwěi*　to have quarreled (cf. P. 5, L. 12)

9 　吁 　　　*syū*　an interjection to signify silence

NOTES

11	風燈	*fēngdēng*	hurricane lamp
12	謙和	*chyānhé*	to be humble or polite

page 21

2	受了委曲	*shòule wěichyu* to have suffered wrong or humiliation
3	插嘴	*chā dzwěi* to butt in, interrupt (a conversation)
4	依舊	*yī jyòu* still, as before
	賭氣	*dǔ chì* to be so angry as to do something reckless out of spite
11	西四牌樓	*Syīszpáilou* name of a street in Peking (lit., West Four Memorial Arches, see P. 79, L. 13)
	胡同	*hútung* lane, alley
	關帝廟	*Gwāndì Myàu* Temple of Kuan, the Divine Emperor. (Kuan Yü 關羽, a famous hero in the period of the Three Kingdoms, third century A. D., was later deified and worshipped as a god of war.)

page 22

3	難住了	*nánjule* to get stuck, stunned
15	省	*shěng* to save, spare

page 23

1	多心	*dwōsyīn* to be suspicious
3	堂客	*tángkè* woman (Peiping colloquial)
7	鬧了一點意見	*nàule yìdyǎn yìjyan* to have shown some difference of opinion, have had a row, have quarrelled
	勸解	*chywànjyě* to reconcile; make peace
11	通知	*tūngjŕ* to notify
12	興高采烈	*syìng gāu tsǎi lyè* in a high spirit, cheerfully
13	板了面孔	*bǎnle myànkǔng* to pull a long face, look displeased

藝 術 家　*Yìshùjyā*

熊佛西　*Syúng Fú-syī*, (1900 -) Playwright. Born in Feng-cheng, Kiangsi. His love of the theatre was revealed very early. While still a student at Yenching University, Peking, he was engaged in the promotion of new drama. After graduating from Yenching in 1923, he came to the United States to study dramatic arts at Columbia University and received his M. A. degree in 1926. After his return to China he was appointed chairman of the Department of Dramatic Arts of the National Peking University and lecturer at his alma mater. In 1932 he became director of the rural theater at Tinghsien, Hopei. After the outbreak of the Sino-Japanese War, he and his troupe of players went to Chengtu, where they gave a series of performances which drew a large audience. Later he became president of the Szechwan Provincial College of Dramatic Arts. After the War, he served as president of the Experimental Dramatic School at Shanghai.

He is one of the pioneers of the new dramatic movement in China. His important works are collected in four volumes. Besides his plays, he is also known for his dramatic criticism.

page 25

　　　藝術家　　*yìshùjyā*　artist

5　　掌櫃　　*jǎnggwèi*　shopkeeper, store-owner (lit., one who is in charge of the shop counter)

7　　作品　　*dzwòpǐn* a literary or artistic work

page 26

4　　哈哈　　*hāhā* ha, ha !

11　　瞧　　*chyáu* to look

　　　兩筆　　*lyǎngbǐ* two strokes(of the writing brush)

NOTES

page 27

1	傑作	*jyédzwò*	masterpiece
2	胡說	*húshwō*	nonsense
3	畫像	*hwà syàng*	to paint a portrait
4	速寫	*sùsyě*	to sketch
	咱們	*dzámen*	we (used only in spoken Chinese when the person spoken to is included)
7	存心	*tswúnsyīn*	to set one's mind on; intentionally, deliberately
9	自討沒趣	*dz̀ tǎu méichyù*	to invite something unpleasant on oneself, get oneself snubbed
12	勞你駕	*láu ni jyà*	if you please; may I trouble you? (a polite expression)
14	調午飯	*tyáu wǔfàn*	to prepare lunch (instead of 調, other words like 烹, 燒, 作 etc. are more generally used.)

page 28

6	拜壽	*bàishòu*	to congratulate a person on his birthday
13	足足	*dzúdzú*	fully
	滿足	*mǎndzú*	to be satisfied
14	浪費	*làngfèi*	to squander
	一文	*yīwén*	a cash, a penny

page 29

5	差	*chāi*	to send (a messenger)
7	假如	*jyǎrú*	if
8	金鋼鑽	*jīngāngdzwàn*	diamond
10	活倒霉	*hwó dǎuméi*	to have bad luck indeed
	窮鬼	*chyúnggwěi*	poor devil (an abusive expression)
12	肉麻	*ròumá*	to cause creepy feelings, be disgusting or nauseating

| 12 | 摩托車 | *mwōtwōchē* | motor car, automobile (摩托 transliteration of motor) |

| 1 | 洋樓 | *yánglóu* | foreign or Western-style building |

| 3 | 綢緞 | *chóu dwàn* | silk and satin |

| 7 | 准 | *jwǔn* | to allow |

| 12 | 十八代的
老祖宗 | *shíbā dài de lǎudzǔdzūng* | an ancestor of the 18th generation back. In quarreling, a Chinese likes to claim himself to be the father or grandfather of his opponent in order to belittle him. Conversely, it would be placating to address one's opponent as "grandfather', "father', etc. |

14	討厭	*tǎuyàn*	to dislike, be disgusted with
	情願	*chíngywán*	to be willing, prefer
	拉洋車	*lā yángchē*	to pull a rickshaw (Rickshaw was introduced to China from Japan, hence a foreign vehicle.)

| 15 | 躲 | *dwǒ* | to hide |
| | 鬼畫 | *gwěihwà* | to paint ghastly, i.e. in a dreadful and ugly manner (鬼 here is an abusive term.) |

| 2 | 幹嗎 | *gànmá* | 作什麼 (cf. P. 12, L. 12) |
| | 禁止 | *jìnjř* | to forbid |

| 3 | 抓住 | *jwāju* | to grab; to hold tightly |
| | 領口 | *lǐngkǒu* | collar˙ |

| 5 | 捏住 | *nyēju* | to pinch |

| 8 | 箝掉 | *chyándyàu* | to clip off with pliers |

| 10 | 棺材 | *gwāntsai* | coffin |

| 11 | 狠狠的 | *hěnhēnde* | fiercely |

NOTES

12	至終	*jìjūng* to the very end, (intensive expression, can be translated here as "just","simply")
	捨不得	*shěbude* to be unwilling to give up
	寶貝畫	*bǎubèihwà* precious drawing (here said sarcastically)
13	拋棄	*pāuchì* to throw away

page 32

1	理想	*lǐsyǎng* ideal
2	活像	*hwósyàng* to be very much like
12	瘋	*fēng* to be crazy

page 33

4	現代	*syándài* contemporary
	第一流	*dìyīlyóu* first rate
6	凡	*fán* all, whoever
	創造	*chwàngdzàu* to create, be creative
	天才	*tyāntsái* genius, talent (lit., inherent ability)
8	古玩舖	*gǔwánpù* curio shop, antique shop
	前無古人	*chyán wú gǔrén* no ancients (i.e. not to be found among the ancients) before you
	後無來者	*hòu wú láijě* no coming generation (i.e., not to be surpassed by any future generation) after you
	畫風	*hwàfēng* style of painting
9	轉機	*jwǎnjī* turning point
	妙處	*myàuchu* the wonderful thing, merit
	傳統的	*chwántǔngde* traditional
	獨闢天地	*dú pì tyāndì* to create a new world by one's self

10	革命的	*gémìngde* revolutionary

12	同事	*túngshr̀* colleagues
	異口同聲	*yì kǒu túng shēng* all with one voice
	稱讚	*chēngdzàn* to praise
	千拜託 萬拜託	*chyān bàitwō, wàn bàitwō* to beg a thousand and ten thousand times; to ask over and over again as a favor

16	瞧你不出	*chyáu ni bùchū* have not looked at you (in this light) i.e. have never figured or expected you to be so good

page 34

3	在某種 條件之下	*dzài mǒujǔng tyáujyan jr̄ syà* under certain conditions

12	馬上	*mǎshàng* immediately
	發財	*fātsái* to get rich

13	嫂嫂	*sǎusau* sister-in-law
	記念	*jìnyàn* to remember, cherish

page 35

4	現洋	*syànyáng* cash; here specifically, silver dollars
	鈔票	*chàupyàu* banknotes; dollar bill

6	掬出	*jyúchu* to grasp, take out

8	代價	*dàijyà* the selling price
	統統	*tūngtūng* all, entirely

12	收入	*shōurù* income

page 36

1	分別	*fēnbye* difference

NOTES

2	人家	*rénjya*	people, others
	恭維	*gūngwei*	to praise, flatter
	祭堂	*jìtáng*	sacrificial hall, funeral parlor
3	輓聯	*wǎnlyán*	a pair of scrolls sent on the occasion of the funeral of a friend or relative.
11	一圓錢	*yīywán chyán*	one dollar (same as 一元 in P. 35, L. 6 or 一塊錢 in P. 36 L. 12)
14	簡直	*jyǎnjŕ*	indeed, simply (an emphatic expression)
	人格	*réngé*	character

page 37

5	倘若	*tǎngrwò*	if
12	絕妙	*jywémyàu*	to be excellent, most wonderful
	照樣	*jàuyàng*	still, in the same way
14	假裝	*jyǎjwāng*	to pretend
15	急症	*jíjèng*	sudden illness, an attack

page 38

2	不妥當	*bùtwǒdang*	to be improper, unsatisfactory
	欺騙	*chīpyàn*	to cheat; deception
	彩色	*tsǎisè*	color, appearance
6	乖	*gwāi*	to be obedient or well-behaved (said of a child)
7	不道德	*búdàudé*	to be immoral
11	墊	*dyàn*	to put something above or in between; to fill up
	氈子	*jāndz*	a carpet, pad
15	罩	*jàu*	to cover
	殘燭	*tsánjú*	burnt-down candles

• 36-38 •

| 16 | 放聲 | *fàngshēng* to raise one's voice |

7	你好狼的心	*nǐ hǎuhěnde syīn* how cruel you are!(See P.10, L. 10.)
8	沒半寸用	*méi bàntswùn yùng* to be so useless
10	突然	*tùrán* suddenly, abruptly
13	天有不測 風雲	*tyān yǒu bútsè fēng yún* in the sky are unpredictable winds and clouds
	人有旦夕 禍福	*rén yǒu dàn syī hwò fú* for a man, his calamity or blessing varies from dawn to evening
15	否則	*fǒudzé* or else, otherwise

| 4 | 包銷 | *bāusyāu* to wrap up (monopolize) the sale of |
| 6 | 有名譽 | *yǒumíngyu* to have fame, be renowned |

3	的確	*díchywè* truly, indeed
	不朽	*bùsyǒu* to be immortal
11	支票	*jīpyàu* check
16	字據	*dz̀jyù* written evidence, receipt

3	畢	*bì* to finish
4	立賣字入	*lì màidz̀ rén* the undersigned seller
4	其兄	*chí syūng* his elder brother
5	當面	*dāng myàn* face to face, in person
	收訖	*shōuchì* received in full

NOTES

5 此據 *tsžjyù* this as evidence or receipt

9 笑容滿臉 *syàurúng mǎn lyǎn* all smiles on one's face

11 畫架 *hwàjyà* an easel

page 43

1 銀行 *yínháng* bank

兌錢 *dwèichyán* to cash money

5 片刻 *pyànkè* in a short while

6 喪事 *sāngshr* funeral

page 44

4 親眼 *chīnyǎn* with one's own eyes

5 經手 *jīngshǒu* to handle; to act as agent

7 憑據 *píngjyu* evidence

15 欽佩 *chīnpèi* to admire, respect

16 歸天 *gweītyān* to pass away (lit., to return to Heaven—a polite expression)

拜見 *bàijyàn* to visit; to pay respects to

page 45

4 台甫 *táifǔ* your honorable name? (a polite expression)

15 打官司 *dǎ gwānsz* to go to court; to have lawsuit

page 46

8 搗 *dǎu* to cause trouble (in expressions such as 搗麻煩, 搗亂)

16 先兄, 亡兄 *syān syūng . . . , wáng syūng* the late deceased elder brother

總而言之 *dzǔng ér yánjr* generally speaking, to state briefly, in short

page 47

6	設身處地	*shè shēn chǔ di*	to put oneself in other's place
	生意	*shēngyi*	business (筆 is used here as a measure for 生意)
	指望	*jǐwàng*	to expect, hope
	叨點光	*tāu dyan gwāng*	to get some advantage or profit
7	殊不知	*shūbùjī*	who would have thought ?
	尋死	*syúnsž*	to commit suicide (lit., to seek death)
	氣死	*chìsž*	to be vexed to death, die of anger
14	虧本	*kwēiběn*	to lose money

page 48

1	簽	*chyān*	to sign
5	丈夫	*jàngfu*	husband
6	慈悲心	*tsźbēisyīn*	pity, merciful heart
7	停會兒	*tíng hwěr*	in a short while
9	無數一次	*wúshù yítsž*	countless times
12	乾脆	*gāntswèi*	to be clear-cut ; straightaway
	就得了	*jyòu déle*	that's all

終身大事 *Jūngshēn Dà Shr̀*

胡　適　　*Hú Shr̀* (1891-1962) Courtesy name : 適之 *Shr̀-jŕ*. Literary critic, poet, and scholar. Born at Chihsi, Anhwei. His father died when he was very young, and, in his boyhood, he lived chiefly under the care of his mother. At 18 he came to the U.S.A. to study, first at Cornell University and later at Columbia University where he receiveed his Ph. D. degree. During these years abroad he gradually developed his ideas of a radical reform in Chinese literature, and formulated them in an epoch-making article entitled 文學改良芻議 *Wénsywé Gǎilyáng Chúyì* (Tentative Suggestions for the Reform of Chinese Literature).

He returned to China in 1917 and for many years taught at various institutions of higher learning. From 1938 to 1942 he was Ambassador to the U. S. A. He went back to China in 1946 to become the Chancellor of the National University of Peking. In 1949 he came back to the States and for ten years made his residence in New York City, pursuing his scholarly studies. He died in Taiwan as President of the Academia Sinica.

He was the first Chinese poet to devote himself to writing poetry exclusively in the spoken language. He was also the first to advocate and promote the use of the vernacular language in literary writings.

page 49

	終身大事	*jūngshēn dà shr̀* the great event in life, i.e., marriage
5	算命先生	*swànmìng syānsheng* fortune-teller
	瞎子	*syādz* blind man
8	沙發榻	*shāfātà* sofa (榻 lit., is a couch.)
9	靠椅	*kàuyǐ* chair, specifically an easy chair on which to recline, to be distinguished from 坐椅, a straight-back chair.
10	靠壁	*kàubì* near the wall, leaning against the wall

寫字檯　　　*syēdżtái*　desk

11　字畫　　　*dżhwà*　calligraphy and painting ; here, it refers to scrolls of these hung on the wall

荷蘭派　　　*Hèlán pài*　Dutch school.　荷蘭 is a transliteration of Holland.

中西合璧　　*jūng syī hé bì*　a combination of Chinese and Weastern styles.　（合璧, lit., means the tallying of two halves of a piece of jade.）

page 50

1　風氣　　　*fēngchi*　fashions, manners　（Cf. expressions such as 風味 P. 66, L. 10 ; 家風 P. 88, L. 11 ; 歐風美雨　P. 89, L. 8.）

2　彈　　　　*tán*　to play on a stringed instrument

絃子　　　*syándz*　string of a musical instrument, a stringed instrument

4　門　　　　*mén*　a measure for 親事 *chīnshr* (marriage, either concluded or being proposed.)

對得　　　*dwèide*　to be agreed on, be well matched

5　據命直言　*jyù mìng jŕ yán*　to speak frankly according to destiny or fortune

10　寅亥巳申　*yín . . . hái . . . sż . . . shēn*　cyclical characters in the twelve 地支 *dìjī*, Terrestrial Branches.　Their positions are 寅 *yín* 3rd, 巳 *sż* 6th, 申 *shēn* 9th, and 亥 *hài* 12th. The symbolic animals are 虎 *hǔ* (tiger) for 寅, 蛇 *shé* (snake) for 巳, 猴 *hóu* (monkey) for 申, and 猪 *jū* (boar) for 亥.　Thus 1950, being 庚寅 *gēngyin*, was the year of the tiger, and 1953, being 癸巳 *gwěisż*, the year of the snake ; 1956, 丙申 *bǐngshēn*, the year of the monkey, 1959, 己亥 *jǐhài*, the year of the boar.

11　配　　　　*pèi*　to match

尅　　　　*kē*　to overcome, destroy

不到頭　　*búdàutóu*　not to reach the end (of natural life), not to come to a good end

合婚   *héhwūn* to make a matrimonial union, marriage

最忌   *dzwèi jì* most tabooed, shunned

12   八字   *bádż* eight cyclic characters, indicating the time of a person's birth:

person's birth: the hour (時辰 *shŕchen*), day, month, and year, each represented by a combination of two characters, one taken from the ten 天干 *tyāngān* Celestial Stems and the other from the twelve Terrestrial Branches. To see whether two people are suitable or not for marriage, a fortune-teller is often consulted. He would arrange and match their eight characters and see if they fit each other.

屬   *shǔ* to belong to, here it means to be born in the year of . . . . Each of the twelve Terrestrial Branches being represented by an animal, a person born in the 亥 year is said to 屬猪.

13   兩重   *lyàngchúng* double, doubly

兩口兒   *lyǎngkǒur* the two of them (Instead of counting heads, the Chinese count by mouths. Thus 人口 means population.)

團圓   *twánywán* to be united (said of members of a family, especially husband and wife)

15   見怪   *jyàngwài* to blame; to take offense

16   觀音娘娘   *Gwānyīn Nyángnyang* Lady Kuan Yin, commonly known as the Goddess of Mercy. She is also called 觀音菩薩 *Gwānyīn Púsa* (P. 51, L. 2), i.e., the Boddhisattva, Kuan Yin.

page 51

3   籤詩   *chyānshŕ* oracular verses, written on yellow paper or bamboo slips 籤. While divination is a specialty of the Taoists, it is also practiced in Buddhist temples.

The poem of four five-character lines that follows is supposed to represent responses from Kuan Yin to the question asked by Mrs. Tyán.

NOTES

3	抽屜	*chōuti* drawers
4	下下	*syàsyà* double-minus. A 下下籤 predicts the worst fortune to the person seeking it.
	前生	*chyánshēng* pre-existence
5	因緣	*yīnywán* affinity, marriage relationship (lit., the cause which produces effects in a future life.)
	莫	*mwò* do not
	強	*chyǔng* by force, against nature or fate
	逆天終有禍	*nì tyān jūng yòu hwò* to act contrary to Heaven brings disaster in the end
8	二十四分	*èrshísì fēn* extremely, very (other expressions are 十分, 十二分, etc : 分 is one tenth of a measure ; hence 十分 or 十二分 represents a full measure or more, while 二十四分 is more than twice a full measure.)
9	合得攏	*hédelǔng* to fit well, be able to go together well (so as to produce a happy union)
12	難爲你	*nánwei ni* to have troubled you ; thanks for the trouble
	對八字	*dwèi bádz̀* to match the eight characters (to see if they can agree on a happy marriage)
13	不用得	*búyùngde* don't have to ; there's no need of it (a polite expression)
	居然	*jyūrán* contrary to expectations ; should have been

page 52

1	柬帖	*jyǎntyē* betrothal card, giving the eight characters
	摺	*jé* to fold
8	請教	*chǐngjyàu* to ask for instruction or advice
9	排排看	*páipai kàn* to arrange and see (if the eight characters match or not)

| 12 | 合不來 | *hébulái* to be unable to get along ; to be ill-matched |

2	同我反對	*túng wǒ fǎndwèi* to be against me, oppose me
3	決斷	*jywédwàn* to make a decision
7	不得已	*bùdéyǐ* no alternative
8	東洋	*dūngyáng* Japan (lit., the east ocean country)
9	爲人	*wéirén* character, behavior
	閱歷	*ywèli* experience
	眼力	*yǎnlì* power of perception, discernment
12	命書	*mìngshū* divination book, fortune-teller's manual
14	遮	*jē* to cover
16	打主意	*dǎjúyi* to make a plan or decision

1	揩	*kāi* to wipe
	淚	*lèi* tears (same as 泪)
4	招呼	*jāuhu* to beckon, greet
6	君子人	*jyūndžrén* gentleman
8	變卦	*byàngwà* change in situation or plan (With a change in 卦 the divination diagram comes a corresponding change in one's fortune and circumstance.)
10	信息	*syìnhsyi* news
16	約摸	*ywēmwo* around, approximately

| 5 | 弄鬼 | *nùnggwěi* to play tricks (弄, also pronounced lùng) |

NOTES

8	盤算	*pánswan* to deliberate, consider
10	發愁	*fāchóu* to become anxious, get worried
11	女壻	*nyǔsyu* son-in-law (壻 is also written as 婿.)
13	子弟	*dẓdì* children, offspring
	留學生	*lyóusywéshēng* a student studying or having studied abroad
14	原配	*ywánpèi* the first wife (lit., the originally betrothed) who is also the legal wife
	休	*syōu* to divorce one's wife
15	一大篇	*yī dà pyān* a whole lot, a great deal

page 56

1	菴	*ān* a small temple, nunnery, or monastery
4	算子罷	*swànle ba* enough of that (see P. 71, L. 15)
7	呸	*pēi* an exclamation of disapproval or contempt
8	泥塑木雕	*ní sù mù dyāu* clay-modelled or wood-caved
13	疑惑	*yíhwo* doubt, misgiving

page 57

4	罪過	*dzwèigwo* how sinful (here used apologetically to mean 'forgive our sins' because Mr. Tyán had dared to say that his wife should have first consulted him instead of the divinities.)
	阿彌陀佛	*ā mī twó fwó* Amitabha Buddha, the invocation of whose name is supposed to bring blessings and atone for sins
5	椿	*jwāng* a measure; used in phrases such as 一 椿 事 情
6	胡說八道	*húshwōbádàu* to talk nonsense
9	虧	*kwēi* thanks to (here used sarcastically for disapproval, Cf. P. 81, L. 16.)

10	害羞	*hàisyōu*	to feel ashamed
	蒙	*méng*	to veil, cover
	一齊通同	*yīchí tūngtúng*	together and united
12	格外	*géwài*	especially, particularly
	慎重	*shènjung*	to be cautious, circumspect
15	迷信	*mísyìn*	superstition, to be superstitious
	正正經經	*jèngjèngjīngjīng*	very seriously

page 58

3	驚慌	*jīnghwāng*	to be startled, alarmed
5	莫非	*mwòfēi* could it be (a conjectural interrogative similar to the expression 是不是.)
6	揀	*jyǎn* to pick, choose. (揀中了 denotes the completion of action with the choice falling on the object.)
7	摸不着頭腦	*mwōbujáu tóunǎu* to be unable to make sense; to be puzzled and bewildered
10	出洋	*chūyáng* to go abroad
	規矩	*gwēijyu* regulations, customs
	祠規	*tsźgwēi* regulations of the ancestral temple
12	犯	*fàn* to offend, violate
16	族譜	*dzúpǔ* a book of family genealogy

page 59

1	結親	*jyéchīn* to be married (same as 結婚 *jyéhwūn,* 成親 *chéngchīn,* 通婚 *tūnghwūn,* etc.)
6	論語	*Lwúnyǔ* the *Analects,* a book containing the sayings of Confucius (Note tone of 論.)

8	陳成子	*Chén Chéngdž* an historical figure who lived in the 5th century B.C. A minister of the feudal state of Ch'i, Chen killed the duke in 481 B.C. This deed incurred the wrath of Confucius, who asked the Duke of Lu to castigate him. See *Analects*, XIV, 22.
9	認定	*rènding* to settle on. to recognize for certainty
12	難道	*nándau* could it be
16	衙門	*yámen* yamen, mandarin's office or court

page 60

1	朝	*cháu* dynasty
	陳友諒	*Chén Yǒulyàng* an historical figure who lived in the 14th century. Originally a fisherman, he became the leader of a rebellion in the last years of the Yüan dynasty and established himself as an emperor in the Yangtze valley. His empire, however, was short-lived and he was soon defeated and killed in battle by the first emperor of the Ming dynasty.
5	革出	*géchū* to be expelled
7	捐	*jywān* to contribute, donate
	罰款	*fákwǎn* fines
8	一直	*yījŕ* a vertical stroke in a character
	拉長	*lācháng* to lengthen, extend
	上下都出了頭	*shàngsyà dōu chūle tóu* the upper and lower ends (of the stroke) both extending out (Thus, by extending the two ends of the central vertical stroke in 田, we have 申.)
9	我當中一直	*wǒ dāngjūng yījŕ* the central vertical stroke in me, i.e., in my family name 田.
10	連累	*lyánlei* to involve, implicate
16	哀告	*āigàu* to plead sadly

page 61

1	罷了	*bàle* all right, no more to be said
2	貪圖	*tāntú* to covet
4	絕望	*jywéwàng* to be hopeless, in despair
	打破	*dǎpwò* to break away from
6	惱	*nǎu* to be displeased with, mad at
	氣頭上	*chìtóushang* at the height of anger
14	隨手	*swéishǒu* right away
16	遞	*dì* to hand to

page 62

1	重	*chúng* again; to repeat
4	匆匆	*tsūngtsūng* hastily
	壓	*yā* to place under or in between something; to press or crush (Cf. P. 66, L. 6.)
8	平平氣	*píngping chì* to calm down one's temper
13	往後一仰	*wàng hòu yìyǎng* to lean or fall back with the face upward
14	眼睜睜的	*yǎn jēngjēngde* with eyes wide-open

回家以後　*Hwéijyā Yǐhòu*

歐陽予倩	*Ōu-yáng Yú-chyàn* (1887-1962) Playwright and actor. Born in Liuyang, Hunan. He for many years devoted himself to the promotion of the theatrical arts in modern China and his numerous plays have exerted a great influence on the new dramatic movement.

page 63

1　登場人名　*dēngchǎng rén míng*: names of persons appearing on stage ; dramatis personae

5　祖母　*dzǔmǔ* grandmother

6　岳父　*ywèfù* wife's father ; similar terms are 岳丈，丈人

8　長工　*chánggūng* manservant or farmhand, regularly employed by the family to work all the year round, to be distinguished from 短工, a day-laborer who does piece work

9　女僕　*nyùpǔ* woman servant, maid

page 64

1　地點　*dìdyǎn* location

4　鄉紳　*syāngshēn* country squire

儉樸　*jyǎnpú* plain, simple, frugal

平房　*píngfáng* one-storey house, (lit., level house)

5　豆棚瓜架　*dòupéng gwājyà* lattice work or trellis for bean and melon vines（瓜 is a generic name for melons, gourds, cucumbers, etc.)

打麥場　*dǎmài chǎng* threshing ground

曬衣叉　*shàiyīchā* clothes-sunning forks ; pronged sticks on which rests a long bamboo pole（竹竿）to serve as clothes-line

6　板凳　*bǎndèng* wooden stool or bench（櫈 is also written as 凳）

7　少奶奶　*shàunǎinai* a form of polite address to a young married woman, or the young mistress of the house

NOTES

8	內應	nèi yīng to answer from inside (the stage)
10	上場	shángchàng to enter (the stage)
	伺候	tsżhou to wait on
	回頭	hwéitóu later (lit., to turn one's head)
12	唯唯	wéiwéi yes, yes
13	自言自語	dżyán dżyǔ to talk to oneself
14	脫了線	twōle syàn the thread has come off
	縫	féng to sew
	無意中	wúyì jūng unitentionally, accidentally

page 65

1	夾層	jyátséng linings
	抽出	chōuchu to take out
	荷花瓣	héhwā bàn lotus petals
	襯	chèn to line
2	唷	yōu an exclamation
	維持	wéichŕ to support, maintain
3	呆了半晌	dāile bànshǎng to be stunned for a while
4	謠言	yáuyan rumor
5	證據	jèngjyu proof, evidence (cf. P.44, L.7)
	海誓山盟	hǎishŕ shānméng swearing by sea and mountain, as pledge of love or fidelity
	吟思	yínsż to meditate (凝思 as in P.74, L.1 is more commonly used.)
6	白切肉	báichyēròu sliced white pork meat, so-called because the meat is boiled in water without being seasoned with salt or soy sauce

7   精神不屬   *jīngshen bùshǔ*   to be dispirited, absent-minded

8   老爺少爺   *lǎuye shàuye*   the elder master and the young master (terms of respect commonly used by servants to refer to the male head of the family and his sons)

       水車   *shwěichē*   a water wheel for irrigation

page 66

1   那不盡然   *ná bújìnrán*   that is not entirely true

       相敬如賓   *syāng jìng rú bīn*   to respect or honor each other like guests (said of husband and wife)

2   作客   *dzwòkè*   to be a guest

3   到處   *dàuchù*   everywhere

6   物質   *wùjŕ*   materialistic

       壓迫   *yāpwò*   to oppress ; oppression

7   別有天地   *byé yǒu tyān dì*   to be in another world or another state of existence

       極其   *jíchí*   extremely, very

       繁華   *fánhwá*   to be gay, gaudy, prosperous

       罪惡   *dzwèiè*   crime, sin

       階級   *jyējí*   class, class distinction

8   指導   *jŕdàu*   to guide, direct

       他   *tā*   here referring to the natural product and simple life mentioned in previous line

10   風味   *fēngwèi*   manners, scenes and delights (lit., 味 means taste or flavor.)

12   宛在目前   *wàn dzài mù chyán*   as if before one's eyes ; appearing vividly

13   油然而生   *yóurán ér shēng*   to ooze like oil ; to rise profusely

NOTES

14	安慰	*ānwei*	to comfort, soothe
15	伴侶	*bànlyǔ*	companion
16	成就	*chéngjyòu*	accomplishment
	學位	*sywéwèi*	academic degree

page 67

1	夠不上	*gòubushàng*	to be not good enough (for you)
6	柔媚	*róumèi*	tenderly and charmingly
9	交際	*jyāujì*	to be sociable ; social intercourse
11	擺架子	*bǎijyàadz*	to put on airs, show off
13	畧緩	*lywè hwǎn*	a bit slowly
	以壯語勢	*yǐ jwàng yǔshr̀*	to give force to one's speech
	情書	*chíngshū*	love letters
15	好頑兒	*hǎuwár*	for fun
16	不相干	*bùsyānggān*	to be unrelated, irrelevant or trivial

page 68

1	露了破綻	*lù le pwòjàn*	to become exposed (lit., to reveal the open seams)
5	公公	*gūnggung*	husband's father
7	幸災樂禍	*syìng dzāi lè hwò*	to rejoice in (other people's) misfortune
	自命	*dzmìng*	to style oneself
	進德會	*jìndéhwèi*	Virtue-promotion Society
	發起人	*fāchǐrén*	founder
8	加油加醬	*jyāyóu jyājyàng*	with a great deal of exaggeration (lit., by adding oil and sauce to give flavor)

8	正直有爲	*jèngjŕ yŏuwéi* to be upright and promising
9	體貼	*tĭtye* to show appreciation and consideration for
	儘管...	*jĭngwǎn* ... *jĭngwǎn* no matter how ... always
	有憑有據	*yŏupíng yŏujyù* with evidence (See P. 44, L. 7)
10	辯論	*byànlwùn* to argue
	良心	*lyángsyin* conscience (lit., good heart)
12	電信	*dyànsyìn* telegrams and letters
13	大少爺	*dà shàuye* the eldest young master (See P. 65, L. 8)
	專人	*jwānrén* special messenger
15	不容	*bùrúng* don't be (lit., do not allow or let yourself)

page 69

6	何況	*hékwàng* furthermore, besides, how much more ! (況 is also written as 况.)
8	苦衷	*kŭjūng* unutterable inner feelings
10	你又來了	*nĭ yòu láile* You are at it again !
	寂寞	*jìmwò* to be lonely
	辜負	*gūfu* to be ungrateful ; to disregard (someone's good intentions, or kindness)
12	以身許之	*yĭ shēn syŭ jŗ̄* to promise to marry (lit., to entrust oneself to someone)

page 70

6	社交	*shèjyāu* social intercouse(See P. 67, L. 9.)
9	言語一科	*yányŭ yìkē* a course in speech (so as to learn to talk glibly)

page 71

1	越…越	*ywè* ... *ywè* the more ... the more

NOTES

6	何嘗	*hécháng* when did I ever (an interrogative phrase implying a negative answer)
7	偶然	*ǒurán* by chance, inadvertently
10	胡鬧	*húnàu* to be improper, reckless (used interchangeably with 糊鬧, P. 97, L. 10)
	情分	*chíngfen* feeling, affection
11	荒唐	*hwāngtang* to be dissolute
13	似乎太過	*sžhu tài gwò* to seem to go too far
	熱鬧塲	*rènau chǎng* gay, bustling arena (of life)
15	俏皮話	*chyàupi hwà* clever, smart talk
	你可以算了吧	*nǐ kéyi swànle ba* that will do for you; that's enough of it
	耽誤	*dānwu* to waste, delay

page 72

3	無可如何	*wú kě rú hé* there is nothing else to be done; to have no way out
6	這下	*jèisyà* this time, right now
	擔…心	*dān . . . syīn* to be worried
	討	*tǎu* to take (a wife)
	洋婆子	*yáng pwódz* a foreign woman (婆子 or 老婆子 is a vulger, sometimes contemptuous, expression for a woman or wife.)
7	度量寬宏	*dùlyang kwānhúng* to be boad-minded (lit., 度 量 means measurement, or capacity)
9	車水	*chē shwěi* to lift water for irrigation by means of a water wheel
11	肚腸子	*dùchángdz* belly and intestines, the viscera

剖　　　　　*pōu* to rip open, dissect

13　那就更妙了　　*nà jyòu gèng myàule* that then would be even more wonderful

14　黑心　　*hēisyīn* wicked heart or consience (lit., black heart)

15　糟了　　*dzāule* too bad !

page 73

1　手段　　*shòudwan* plot, method, underhanded way

4　灌　　*gwàn* to pour down ; to make a person take liquids (such as medicine, wine)

迷魂湯　　*míhwúntāng* love potion (lit., soul-bewitching soup)

7　暗算了去　　*ánswánle chyù* to be secretly plotted against ; to be harmed secretly

8　翻壇打廟　　*fāntán dǎmyàu* to create disturbance ; act riotously (lit., to overturn the altar and to fight in the temple)

淘氣　　*táuchì* to be naughty or mischievous

10　她要萬一趕了來　　*tā yàu wànyī gǎnle lái* if by chance she should overtake me here

16　耳語　　*ěryǔ* to whisper (lit., to talk with mouth close to listener's ear)

page 74

1　端　　*dwān* to bring, hold (dish, tray)

4　手勢　　*shǒushr̀* gesture

7　招招手　　*jāujau shou* to beckon with hand

蓮子羹　　*lyándž gēng* lotus-seed soup

8　會意　　*hwèiyì* to take the hint

勉強　　*myanchyǎng* to be constrained, unwilling, forced

NOTES

8	張着口	*jāngje kŭu* to open one's mouth
10	爲難	*wéinán* to be in difficulty, embarrassing
	親手	*chīnshŏu* with one's own hands
12	不屑	*búsyè* to consider as unworthy, be contemptuous of
13	膽兒	*dănr* courage
15	孝順	*syàushwun* to be filial to, serve (parents)

page 75

3	荷葉	*héyè* lotus leaves
5	大吃一驚	*dà chī yìjīng* to be greatly surprised
8	蓮蓬	*lyánpeng* seed case of the lotus
15	黃鼠狼	*hwángshŭláng* weasel

page 76

4	大都會	*dà dūhwèi* big cities, metropolis
6	大頭菜	*dàtóutsài* salted turnips
10	妖怪	*yāugwai* monster
11	回頭	*hwéitóu* later, in the end
15	志在四方	*jr̀ dzài sz̀ fāng* one's ambition is in the four quarters

page 77

2	光燦燦	*gwāngtsăntsăn* to be shiny, glittering
3	彷彿	*făngfu* as if
5	仰天	*yăngtyān* to look up towards heaven
	轉過來	*jwănwolai* to be turned back or restored to life
6	跟踪兒上似的	*gēndzūngr shàng szde* as if pursuing
	膀子	*băngdz* the upper arm

9	胡思亂想	*húsz̄ lwànsyǎng* frenzied and confused thoughts; to be delirious
10	囉囉索索	*lwōlwōswōswō* prattling; to talk boringly
12	乂開	*chǎkāi* to turn aside
14	姻伯母	*yīnbwómŭ* elder aunt (through marriage connection)
15	親家	*chìngjya* title of address used by parents of married couples to each other (Note pron. of 親.)

page 78

1	轉述	*jwǎnshù* to repeat; to report what has been said
	周旋	*jōusywan* to wait on; to engage in friendly conversation
2	成了人	*chéngle rén* to be grown-up
	我人	*wǒ rén* my health (lit., my person)
	肝氣	*gānchì* air in the liver, supposed to produce anger and other indispositions
15	糠糕	*dzāugāu* to be muddled. messed up. spoiled (See P. 72, L. 15.)
16	世道人心	*shr̀dàu rénsyīn* the way of the world and the mind of men, i.e., manners, morals, and public opinions
	測	*tsè* to fathom, predict
	中流砥柱	*jūng lyóu dǐ jù* an immovable rock in midstream; cf. English expression 'pillar of society'
	挽回	*wǎnhwéi* to pull back; to reform
	頹風	*twéifēng* decadent morals, depraved manners

page 79

1	大有可爲	*dà yǒu kě wéi* to be able to do lots of things; to be very promising

NOTES

2   司務   *sūwù* servant, cook, etc. (lit., one in charge of household work)

4   嘗嘗   *chángchang* to taste

6   疼   *téng* to love passionately, to be very fond of

7   作針線   *dzwò jēnsyan* to do needlework, sew

8   撐持   *chēngchŕ* to prop up, support

    拔貢   *bágùng* to be promoted to senior licentiate, i.e. to succeed in passing the preliminary civil service examina tion for the third degree

    法政學堂   *fǎjéng sywétáng* school of law and political science, (a Western-type school)

13   豎牌樓   *shù páilou* to erect memorial arch (in commemoration of outstanding virtue such as loyalty, chastity, filial piety; no longer in vogue after China became republic)

14   請示   *chǐng shŕ* to ask for instruction or advice

15   官費   *gwānfèi* government scholarship

15   空名聲   *kūng míngsheng* vain reputation

page 80

1   於心無愧   *yú syīn wúkwèi* without being ashamed at heart

    本事   *běnshr* ability

    依傍   *yībàng* something to lean on, a prop

3   閉得口眼   *bìde kǒuyǎn* to be able to close mouth and eyes (upon death), i.e., to die without regret

4   長輩   *jǎngbèi* elders, those of a generation above

5   獨子   *dúdž* only son

    溺愛不明   *nìài bùmíng* to dote on blindly; to spoil

11   寒士   *hánshŕ* poor students or scholars

| 15 | 討親 | *tǎuchīn* to get a wife (See P. 72, L. 6.) |

| 1 | 該死 | *gāisž* to be damned |

| 4 | 何不 | *hébù* why not |

| 8 | 經不起風浪 | *jīngbuchǐ fēnglàng* to be unable to stand the storms |

| 10 | 敬幾杯 | *jìng jibēi* to offer a few cups (of wine) |

| 13 | 喜酒 | *syǐjyǒu* a feast, celebrating some happy family occasion such as birth of a child, wedding, etc. |

| 14 | 斟 | *jēn* to pour (drink) |

| | 上菜 | *shàngtsài* to bring up dishes, serve dishes |

| | 請酒 | *chǐngjyǒu* to invite (each other) to drink; to toast |

| 16 | 多虧 | *dwō kwēi* to depend mainly on, owe a great deal to, be much indebted to |

| | 先君 | *syān jyūn* my late father |

| 9 | 令媛 | *lìng ywán* your daughter, a polite form of address |

| 10 | 癖性 | *pǐsying* peculiar habit, addicted nature, special fondness for something |

| 14 | 暢快 | *chàngkwai* to be happy, joyful |

| | 暢飲 | *chàngyǐn* to drink joyfully without restraint |

| 16 | 印證 | *yìnjèng* to verify or confirm |

| 1 | 從新 | *tsúngsyīn* anew |

| | 翻檢 | *fānjyǎn* to search out and examine |

| 2 | 積累 | *jīlěi* to accumulate successively |

| 4 | 車水馬龍 | *chē shwěi mǎ lúng* carriages like flowing water and horses like dragons—a phrase used to describe the gaiety of city life with its endless stream of traffic |

NOTES

4	受用	*shòuyùng*	to be enjoyable
5	鈎心鬥角	*gōu syīn dòu jyǎu*	to be intriguing and contentious, scheming
	競爭	*jìngjēng*	competition ; to compete
6	絕大的	*jywédàde*	exceedingly huge
	漩渦	*sywánwō*	whirlpool
7	頗	*pwō*	very, quite ; 頗 爲 is same as 很 是.
	沉痛中肯	*chéntùng jūngkěn*	to be painfully true and point-blank
9	不然	*bùrán*	not so, no
11	弄得…爲止	*nùngde . . . wéi jř*	to become . . . in the end, end up in . . . .
	莫明其妙	*mwò míng chí myàu*	to be in a dilemma, uncertain (lit., not to understand the mystery)
12	幻境	*hwànjìng*	visionary world, land of illusions
13	往往	*wǎngwǎng*	often
	支配	*jīrpèi*	to control
14	懷疑	*hwáiyí*	misgiving, suspicion ; to suspect
16	引誘	*yǐnyòu*	temptation ; to tempt

page 84

1	搗亂	*dǎulwàn*	to cause trouble or agitation
3	無可掩飾	*wú kě yǎnshr̀*	to be unable to conceal or cover up
6	素菜	*sùtsài*	vegetable dish, (to be distinguished from 葷菜, meat dish)
8	方才	*fāngtsái*	just now
9	貿易公司	*máuyi gūngsz̄*	trading company

10	定期船	*dìngchī chwán*	a passenger boat that sails on a regular schedule
13	許	*syŭ*	same as 也許 perhaps
16	有是有過	*yŏu shr̀ yŏugwo*	yes, there had been (an emphatic way of speech, usually followed by a 可是 clause)

page 85

1	迫不及待	*pwò bùjí dài*	so urgent that it could hardly wait or be delayed
3	泡菜	*pàutsài*	pickled vegetable, vegetable soaked in salt water until tasty
4	鎮定	*jènding*	to calm down
6	交涉	*jyāushè*	negotiation, transaction
12	下米	*syàmǐ*	to put rice in pot to cook
	翩然	*byānrán*	fluttering
14	稟明	*bǐngmíng*	to inform; to report (to a superior)

page 86

2	暮年	*mùnyán*	declining years, old age
3	絆住	*bànju*	to detain, hinder
	前程	*chyánchéng*	future career (lit., the road ahead)
	無限	*wúsyàn*	to be unlimited
4	流戀	*lyóulyàn*	to yearn; to have lingering affection for
	骨肉	*gǔròu*	members of one's family; kindred or children (lit., bone and flesh)
	餘光	*yúgwāng*	lingering light
5	慷慨	*kǎngkài*	to be generous or noble-hearted
	義烈	*yìlyè*	to be righteous and high-minded

NOTES

5   女丈夫   *nyū jàngfu*   a great and outstanding woman (lit., a man among women)

      圖   *tú*   to desire, plan

6   置大恩於 不顧   *jr̀ dà ēn yú búgù*   to disregard or forget entirely (other's) great kindness

8   顯親揚名   *syǎn chīn yáng míng*   to bring glory and fame to one's parents

      承歡色笑   *chéng hwān sè syàu*   to give delight (to one's parents) by watching their looks and smiles

      漸說漸走   *jyàn shwō jyàn dzǒu*   to talk while walking

      同席   *hwéisyí*   to go back to one's seat at the table

9   甜菜   *tyántsài*   a sweet dish usually served at the end of a formal meal

16   耳刮子   *ěrgwādz*   a slap on the ear or side of the face

page 87

2   遊歷   *yóulì*   to travel

5   不知所可   *bù jr̄ swǒ kě*   not knowing what to do; to be ill at ease

10   家嚴   *jyāyán*   my father

      外子   *wàidž*   my husband

13   敗類   *bàilèi*   worthless fellow, knave (lit., bad species)

      害人的賊   *hàirénde dzéi*   pernicious thief, villain

      千方百計   *chyānfāng bǎijì*   with all kinds of tricks

16   動手   *dùngshǒu*   to start, to begin

page 88

1   腐敗   *fǔbài*   to be corrupt, decadent

2   上當   *shàng . . . dàng*   to be deceived by

2	妾	*chyè*	concubine
3	無從	*wútsúng*	no way to
	經營	*jīngyíng*	to manage
	煤礦	*méikwàng*	coal mine
5	敷衍	*fūyan*	to humor ; to win over to friendliness
7	縣知事	*syàn jīshr̀*	county magistrate
8	一生一世	*yìshēng yíshr̀*	in one's entire life, during a lifetime
	軟弱無能	*rwǎnrwò wúnéng*	to be weak and incompetent
11	家風	*jyāfēng*	family morals or reputation
	到這步田地	*dàu jèibu tyándì*	to such an extent or degree (here 步 is a measure.)
13	憤極而悲	*fènjí ér bēi*	to become distressed with rage
14	溜	*lyōu*	to slip out
16	發怔	*fālèng*	to be stunned or agitated
	咬咬耳朵	*yǎuyau ěrdwo*	to whisper to the ear (lit., to bite the ears)

page 89

4	擠上	*jǐshang*	to push through a crowd, push forward
5	和盤託出	*hépán twōchū*	to reveal completely (lit., to bring out the whole tray)
6	懺悔	*chànhwěi*	confession, repentance
7	不禁	*bújìn*	cannot help or refrain from
	歐風美雨	*Ōufēng Měiyǔ*	the morals and manners of Europe and America, i.e., Western cultural influences (here, 風 and 雨 are used figuratively)
	浸潤	*chìnrwùn*	to be immersed in or nourished by
9	顧盼	*gùpàn*	regard, attention

NOTES

9	此番	*tsžfān* this time

10	愕然	*èrán* to be startled
	握拳	*wò chywán* to clench one's fists
	無窮	*wúchyúng* to be endless, inexhaustible

page 90

1	有氣沒力的	*yǒuchì méilì de* weakly or dispiritedly (lit., with breath but without strength)
2	變遷	*byànchyān* change
3	還成人嗎	*hái chéng rén ma* Can one still be considered a man?
4	麻木不仁	*mámù bùrén* to be benumbed and insensible
5	不莊重	*bùjwāngjung* to be undignified
	無賴	*wúlài* to be shameless
	豈有此理	*chǐ yǒu tsž lǐ* to be absurd (lit., how could there be such reason or logic?)
6	廉恥	*lyánchř* sense of shame
7	遺產	*yíchǎn* inheritance
8	詩書禮義	*shř shū lǐ yì* poetry, history, rites, and righteousness
	破產	*pʊʊchǎn* to be bankrupt
10	歸	*gwei* to belong to, come under
	管束	*gwǎnshù* control; to discipline
11	資格	*džge* qualification
	目下	*mùsyà* right now; at present
12	說白話	*shwō báihwà* to speak empty or useless words, talk nonsense
15	墮落	*dwòlè* fall, degeneration

15 關鍵 *gwānjyàn* pivot or key (to a situation), critical moment

page 91

1 就今天而論 *jyòu jīntyan ér lwùn* so far as the present is concerned; (lit., 就 . . . 而 論 means : taking . . . into consideration)

質問 *jŕwèn* to interrogate, cross-examine, question

2 在父執之列 *dzài fùjŕ jŕ lyè* in the rank of father's friends, among father's friends

措詞失當 *tswòtsź shŕdàng* to be improper in wording or remarks

狂忘無稽 *kwángwàng wújī* to be arrogant and unfounded, (妄 should be used instead of 忘.)

3 髮妻 *fǎchī* first wife (to whom one is betrothed in childhood when the hair is first put up)

5 分明 *fēnmíng* clearly, evidently

6 公然 *gūngrán* publicly

7 當初 *dāngchū* in the beginning, at that time

8 草率 *tsǎushwài* be careless, hasty

9 贊同 *dzàntúng* to approve

11 半開化 *bàn kāihwà* to be half-civilized

信用 *syìnyung* credit

12 甚至於 *shènjŕyu* even

放過 *fànggwò* to let go easily

裝腔 *jwāngchyāng* to pretend or affect innocence (lit., to sing in a falsetto voice)

page 92

1 獎勵 *jyǎnglì* to encourage

贖罪 *shúdzwèi* to atone for sins

NOTES

3	薄倖	*bwósyìng*	to be lacking in affection, heartless
4	例外	*lìwài*	to be exceptional ; exceptic n
	要求	*yāuchyóu*	request ; to demand
5	擱一擱	*gēyigē*	to put aside for a moment
	人生觀	*rénshēnggwān*	view of life, philosophy of life
6	交換	*jyāuhwàn*	to exchange ; reciprocally
	處置	*chǔjr̀*	to deal with, dispose of
9	縱然	*dzùngrán*	even though
	不足齒數	*bùdzú chř̌shù*	to be of no consequence, unimportant, not worth considering
	不妨	*bùfáng*	might as well
10	操勞	*tsāuláu*	to bear hardship, toil
12	補救於萬一	*bǔjyòu yú wànyī*	to be repaired or redeemed in the slightest degree (lit., one ten thousandth)
15	輕侮	*chīngwǔ*	to be disdainful, contemptuous
	淡漠	*dànmwò*	to be indifferent, apathetic

page 93

2	避開	*bìkāi*	to keep away, get out of the way
	怠慢	*dàimàn*	to be disrespectful to, treat rudely
3	支吾	*jr̄wu*	to prevaricate; to evade the issue
4	絕對	*jywédwèi*	absolutely
	監督	*jyāndū*	supervision
5	狡獪	*jyǎugwài*	craftiness, trick
6	利害	*lìhai*	to be harsh, terrible (厲害 is more commonly used)

6	遲疑	*chíyí* to hesitate
	把當給人上	*bǎ dàng gěi rén shàng* to play tricks on people (cf.P.88, L.2)
9	怪相	*gwàisyàng* funny face
12	馬馬糊糊	*māmāhūhū* without special effort, casually
	混過	*hwùngwò* to muddle through
13	搖彩票	*yáu tsǎipyàu* to draw lottery
	頭彩	*tóutsǎi* first prize
16	下臺	*syàtái* to get out of a predicament (lit., to get off the stage)
	大方	*dàfang* to be stately, graceful

page 94

5	局外人	*lyúwàirén* outsider
	誠懇	*chéngkěn* to be earnest
13	境界	*jìngjyè* scene, environment
	容得下	*rúngdesyà* to be able to hold or contain
14	哄騙	*hǔngpyàn* to deceive
16	煞風景	*shāfēngjǐng* to spoil the beautiful scene or view; to make unpleasant

page 95

4	顧全	*gùchywán* to look after the welfare of, care for
5	倉促之間	*tsāngtsù jī jyān* in a great hurry
6	結伴同行	*jyébàn túngsyíng* to accompany each other, go together
9	過時	*gwòshŕ* to be behind time or out-of-date
	解鈴繫鈴	*jyě líng syì líng* to loosen the bell that has been tied on (a tiger's) neck, i.e., to get out of a difficult situation into which one has got

NOTES

10	了結	*lyǎujyé* to conclude
12	履行	*lyǔsyíng* to fulfill

page 96

6	卑劣	*bǐlyè* to be mean, despicable
	煙霧漫天	*yānwù màn tyān* to be confused and muddled (lit., smoke and fog filling the sky)
	光景	*gwāngjing* condition, state of things
7	野人	*yěrén* savages
8	出頭	*chūtóu* to emerge (from poverty and obscurity); to come to the front
9	氣得上氣 不接下氣	*chìde shàngchì bùjyē syàchì* to be so angry as to be out of breath
12	放明白	*fàng míngbai* to get to understand
	休	*syōu* should never
	轉灣	*jwǎnwār* to turn round; to shift one's position or attitude
	羅網	*lwówǎng* net, trap
16	拚	*pīn* to stake, risk; 我 一 生 拚 給 你 了 I'll stake my whole life against you.

page 97

1	顫動	*chàndùng* to tremble
3	辛辛苦苦	*syīnsyīnkǔkǔ* with much trouble and hardship
8	自此	*dz̀ tsž* henceforth, from now on
9	好說話	*hǎushwōhwà* to be affable, easy to get along with
10	寬容	*kwānrúng* to tolerate, forgive
11	你於心何忍	*mǐ yú syīn hé rěn* how can you be so hard-hearted, unfeeling

11	恢復	*hwēifu* to restore, regain
13	關連	*gwānlyán* connection
14	懦弱	*nwòrwò* to be weak and cowardly

page 98

4	無所不至	*wú swǒ bú jr̀* there is nothing that is not done ; to go all the way
6	慚愧	*tsánkwèi* to be ashamed
8	停妻再娶	*tíng chī dzài chyǔ* to divorce and marry again (Here, it seems to mean to keep one's wife and marry another at the same time.)
11	檢點	*jyǎndyǎn* to examine, check
12	舅姑	*jyòugū* husband's parents
13	養蠶	*yǎngtsán* to raise silkworm
14	方寸	*fāngtswín* the heart (supposed to be the size of a square inch), a limited sphere
15	隣居	*línjyū* neighbor

page 99

1	傷心	*shāngsyīn* to be grieved, broken-hearted
	娛	*yú* to entertain ; to cheer up
4	決裂	*jywélyè* to break up relations
7	乞憐	*chǐlyán* to beg for sympathy
8	苦楚	*kǔchǔ* pain, painful experience
9	荳棚瓜架	*dòupéng gwājyà* Here the expression is used figuratively to denote a simple rural life (cf note, P.64, L.5)
	不適於	*búshr̀yú* to be not suitable for

NOTES

9   金迷紙醉   *jīn mí jǐ dzwèi* to be dazzled by gold and intoxicated with paper (It is said figuratively of one who indulges in extravagance and luxury. The story is told of one Meng Fu, an imperial physician, who fled the capital to make his home in Szechuan during the last years of the T'ang dynasty. There he built a house in which there was a small room with bright windows and all the vessels and utensils made of shiny gold paper. A relative who visited it came out to tell his friends: "When I rested in this room, I was dazzled by the gold and intoxicated with the paper.")

     錦繡   *jǐnsyòu* embroidery; to be elegant

16   品行   *pǐnsying* conduct, morals

page 100

4   消滅   *syāumyè* to erase, obliterate

     限量   *syànlyàng* to limit; to measure or estimate (See 無限 P. 86, L. 3.)

     南極   *nánjí* the South Pole

     探險   *tànsyǎn* to explore; exploration

5   談助   *tánjù* topic for conversation, conversation piece

8   徹底   *chèdǐ* thoroughly

9   鞠躬   *jyúgūng* to bow

11   乘   *chèng* to ride (here used as a measure for sedan-chair, carriage, etc.)

16   湊近   *tsòujìn* to come closer

page 101

3   驚動   *jīngdùng* to disturb

5   無精打采   *wú jīng dǎ tsǎi* dispiritedly

教我如何不想!她　*Jyàu　Wǒ　Rúhé　Bùsyǎng　Tā*

劉　復　　*Lyóu　Fù* (1889-1934) Poet and philologist. Born in
Kiangyin, Kiangsu. He received his Ph. D. from the
University of Paris. After returning to China, he became
professor in the Department of Chinese Literature,
National University of Peking; chairman of the Depart-
ment of Chinese Literature, Université Franco-Chinoise;
dean of the Women's College of Arts and Sciences,
National Peking University; director of studies, Fu
Jen University. In 1934, he died at Peking after a
tour in Suiyuan Province to study the dialects there.

His two volumes of poems won him fame as a leading
poet during the early years of the Chinese Renaissance
and contributed to the promotion of the 白話 *pái hwà*
(vernacular) poetry. In his last years, he was engaged
in a movement to unify the Chinese national language.

page 105

1　飄　　　*pyāu* to float

6　戀愛　　*lyànài* to love (usually between man and woman)

9　蜜　　　*mì* honey

　　銀夜　　*yín yè* silvery night

page 106

6　枯樹　　*kū shù* withered trees

7　野火　　*yě hwǒ* wild fire, prairie fire

　　暮色　　*mù sè* twilight, sunset

NOTES

一 笑 *Yi Syàu*

page 108

1　情詩　　*chíngshr̄* love poems

2　境地　　*jìngdì* situation

5　也罷　　*yě bà* all right, very well (the line can be translated as "no matter whether it is joyful or sad")

7　不曾　　*bùtséng* have not yet

詩的宣言　*Shīde Sywānyán*

郭沫若　*Gwō Mwò-rwò* (1892 -) Poet and critic. Born in Loshan, Szechwan. He studied medicine in Japan and wrote many poems while at the the university there. After returning to China, he organized in 1922 together with his friends the 'Creative Society', which became one of the most influential literary associations at that time. In 1925 he went to Canton to become dean of the College of Arts and Letters at the National Sun Yat-sen University. After the split of the Kuomintang and the Communist party in 1927, he returned to Shanghai, where he devoted himself to the promotion of proletarian literature. When the situation became intolerable for the left wingers, he fled to Japan, where he stayed until the outbreak of the Sino-Japanese War. He then returned to China and served as the head of the Third Department of the Ministry of Political Training, and later, chairman of the Committee for the Promotion of Cultural Activities. He visited U.S.S.R. in 1945, and attended the Political Consultative Conference as a non-party delegate in January, 1946. Now he is president of the Academy of Sciences in Communist China.

page 109

宣言　*sywānyán* manifesto, statement, announcement

1　眞率　*jēnshwài* genuine, naive

2　修飾　*syōushr̄* adornment

4　赤腳　*chr̄ jyǎu* to bare feet ; to be barefooted

　裸　*lwǒ* to be naked

6　仇視　*chóushr̀* to regard as enemy, be hostile

8　綾羅　*línglwó* silk, gauze

page 110

4　鍛鍊　*dwànlyàn* discipline, training (lit., to smelt, to refine)

8　怒吼　*nùhǒu* to roar with rage

NOTES

徐志摩　*Syú Jř-mwó* (1896-1931) Poet. Born in Haining, Chekiang. After graduation from the National University of Peking he came to study banking at Columbia University, where he received his M.A. degree. He then went to England and studied economics and political science at Cambridge University, writing many poems in his spare time. As a pioneer in modern Chinese poetry, he broke away from tradition and created new poetic forms of his own. He taught in several universities and in 1928 organized the 新月社 *Syīnywè Shè* (Crescent Society) with 胡適 *Hú Shř*, 聞一多 *Wén Yī-dwō*, and others, and publihed the 新 月 月 刊 (Crescent Monthly) as its organ. He was killed in August 1931 in an airplane accident near Tsinan, Shantung.

page 111

1	雪花	*sywěhwā* snowflake
2	翩翩	*pyānpyān* to be fluttering
	瀟洒	*syāusǎ* to be light and free
4	飛颺	*fēiyáng* to fly, soar
6	冷寞	*lěngmwò* to be cold and solitary
	幽谷	*yōugǔ* lonely, shaded valley
7	淒清	*chīchīng* to be mournful and desolate
	山麓	*shānlù* foot of a hill
8	荒街	*hwāng jyē* deserted street
	惆悵	*chóuchàng* to be mournful, disappointed

page 112

| 1 | 娟娟 | *jywānjywān* gracefully |

5	硃砂梅	*jūshāméi* a kind of flowering plum tree with vermilion-colored blossoms
6	憑藉	*píngjyè* to rely on
7	盈盈	*yíngyíng* lightly and gracefully
	沾住	*jānjù* to cling to, stick firmly on
	衣襟	*yījīn* dress, lapel of a garment
8	貼近	*tyējìn* to keep close to
	柔波	*róu bwō* gentle waves, ripples
9	消溶	*syāurúng* to melt

NOTES

閩一多先生的書桌　　*Wén Yīdwō Syānshengde Shūjwō*

閩一多　　*Wén Yīdwō* (1899-1946) Poet, painter, and scholar. Born in Hupeh. After an education at Tsinghua University in Peking, he came to study in the U.S.A. Since his return to China in 1925, he had taught at a number of universities, including his alma mater, as professor of Chinese literature. He came early under the influence of the New Poetry movement and published his first volume of poems when he was a student. In his later years he was known as a literary historian and poetic critic, in which capacity he succeeded in bringing form and meter to the new poetry. He was also an intense patriot. During the Sino-Japanese war, he moved with the university to Kunming, where he emerged from his peaceful scholarly retreat as a champion for new democracy. His political activities ultimately cost him his life when he was assassinated in Kunming shortly after the war. His complete works were collected and edited by his friends in four volumes in 1948.

page 113

1　靜物　　*jìngwù* still life

2　怨聲　　*ywànshēng* murmuring, complaining voice

　　騰沸　　*téngfèi* to rise loudly ; to bubble and boil (denoting confusion and unrest)

3　墨盒　　*mwòhé* ink box, (usually a small bronze box with black ink-soaked silk cotton)

4　字典　　*dзdyǎn* dictionary

　　漬濕　　*dзshī* to soak ; to wet thoroughly

5　信箋　　*syìnjyān* letter paper

　　彎痛　　*wāntùng* to bend until it hurts

6　煙灰　　*yānhwēi* cigarette ashes

　　閉塞　　*bìsài* to close ; to stop up

• 113 •

7	毛筆	*máubǐ* writing brush
	火柴	*hwǒchái* matches
	燒禿	*shāutū* to burn until bald
8	抱怨	*bàuywan* to complain

page 114

1	香爐	*syānglú* incense-burner
	咕嚕	*gūlou* to mumble
	野蠻	*yěmán* to be savage, unruly
2	定規	*dìnggwei* surely
	擠倒	*jǐdǎu* to push down (because of crowding)
3	鋼錶	*gāngbyǎu* steel watch
	銹	*syòu* to rust
4	稿紙	*gǎujǐ* manuscript sheets
5	筆洗	*bǐsyǐ* a bowl with water for cleaning the writing brush
	盛	*chéng* to hold
6	臭辣	*chòulà* to be stinking and acrid
	雪茄灰	*sywějyāhwēi* cigar ashes
8	墨水壺	*mwòshwěihú* ink bottle

page 115

3	狼狽	*lángbèi* to be disorderly and distressing
5	鮫	*yǎu* to hold with teeth; to bite (same as 咬)
	迷迷地笑	*mímíde syàu* to smile gently
6	眾生	*jùngshēng* all living things
	各安其位	*gè ān chí wèi* each to hold its proper place, each satisfied with its position
7	糟塌	*dzāuta* to waste or spoil
8	秩序	*jìsyu* order

NOTES

謝冰心   *Syè Bīng-syīn* (1902 -) Short-story writer, poet and essayist. Born in a family of official rank and fine traditions in Minhou, Fukien. She spent her childhood in Yentai (Chefoo), Shantung, where the beautiful scenery of the sea made upon her young mind a deep impression, which was not infrequently reflected in her works later on. She graduated from Yenching University in 1923 and received her master's degree from Wellesley College in 1926. She was professor of literature at Yenching until the outbreak of the Sino-Japanese War. During the war years, she became a member of the People's Political Council. After the war she was in Japan for sometime before she returned finally to mainland China.

page 116

     繁星   *fánsyīng* numerous stars

1   閃爍   *shǎnshwò* to gleam

2   太空   *tàikūng* great void, sky

7   嫩綠   *nènlyù* tender green

9   發展   *fājǎn* to develop

12   貢獻   *gùngsyàn* to offer, contribute

page 117

3   犧牲   *syīshēng* to sacrifice

8   灑遍   *sǎbyàn* to scatter (water) all over

我是一條小河　*Wǒ Shr̀ Yītyáu Syǎu Hé*

馮至　　　*Féng Jr̀* （1905 -) Poet and essayist. Born in Hopei. He is a returned student from Germany, a teacher of German literature, and author of several volumes of poems and essays. As a poet, his main contribution is the introduction of the sonnet form to modern Chinese poetry. During the Sino-Japanese War he lived in Kunming, where he taught at the National Southwest Associated University. After the war he returned to Peking and was professor at the National University of Peking, which positon he still holds. His latest work is *A Biography of Tu Fu*, published in 1952. A selection of his poems and essays appeared in 1955.

page 118

2　　無心　　　*wú syīn* unintentionally

　　　繞過　　　*ràugwò* to pass around

3　　彩霞　　　*tsǎisyá* colored clouds

4　　輭輭　　　*rwǎnrwǎn* to be gentle, soft （same as 軟）

5　　森林　　　*shēnlín* forest

6　　蕩蕩　　　*dàngdàng* to ripple ; to flow back and forth

7　　碧翠　　　*bìtswèi* green （like emerald）

8　　裁剪　　　*tsáijyǎn* to cut out

　　　裙裳　　　*chyúnshāng* skirt

page 119

1　　花叢　　　*hwātsúng* flowery grove

2　　粼粼　　　*línlín* to be crystal clear

NOTES

3	悽豔	*chīyàn*	to be sadly beautiful
4	編織	*byānjŕ*	to weave
	花冠	*hwāgwān*	a flower wreath or crown
5	無奈呀	*wú nài ya*	alas! (i.e., there is no alternative)
	終於	*jūngyú*	after all, finally
8	擊碎	*jīswèi*	to break to pieces
9	漂漾	*pyāuyàng*	to float, drift
12	幻散	*hwànsàn*	to disperse like an illusion

過 橋　*Gwò Chyáu*

李廣田　*Lǐ Gwǎng-tyán* (1907 -) Poet, story writer, and literary critic. He was born in a farming family in Shantung and brought up amid rural surroundings. He graduated from the Department of Western Languages and Literatures of the National University of Peking. In 1936, he published together with his former school-mates 何其芳 *Hé Chí-fāng* and 卞之琳 *Byàn Jī-lín* a volume of poetry entitled *The Garden of Han*. Both during and after the Sino-Japanese War he taught in a number of universities. His writings have appeared frequently in different magazines and newspapers.

page 120

2	遊戲	*yóusyì* to play
3	踢碎	*tīswèi* to kick asunder
	珍珠露	*jēnjūlù* pearly dews
	駐	*jù* to halt ; to stand still
5	蝃蝀在東	*dídùng dzài dūng* The rainbow is in the east (蝃蝀 or 螮蝀 is an archaic poetic expression for 虹 rainbow. The quotation is from the *Classic of Poetry*, poem no. 51.)
7	啞	*yǎ* to be dumb, silent
8	跨過	*kwàgwò* to stride across
	一控	*yíkùng* (like) a bow

page 121

2	樂園	*lèywán* paradise
6	原野	*ywányě* wilderness
8	默默	*mwòmwò* silently
	攜手	*syīshǒu* hand in hand

NOTES

望 *Wàng*

卞之琳   *Byàn Jī-lín* (1910 -) Poet. Born in Kiangsu near the estuary of the Yangtze River. He graduated from the National University of Peking in 1933 when the first collection of his poems was published. Some of them had appeared in the *Crescent Monthly* where his fame as a translator was already well established. In 1938 he travelled to the Northwest and lived among the guerrillas for two years. This experience enriched the stories, essays, and poems he wrote during the war years. Besides teaching in universities, he has translated and edited a number of translations from western literature. He is known as one of the best among the Chinese poets today.

page 122

1	晴空	*chíngkūng*	clear sky
2	地圖	*dìtú*	map
3	一朵朵	*yīdwǒdwǒ*	in clusters
4	洲	*jōu*	continent
	島嶼	*dǎuyǔ*	islands, small and large
5	大陸	*dàlù*	mainland, continent
	山嶺	*shānlǐng*	mountain ranges
6	孔隙	*kǔngsyī*	hollows
	裂縫	*lyèfèng*	cracks
	冷落	*lěnglè*	to be lonely
8	港灣	*gǎngwān*	harbors and bays
	帆	*fān*	sail

page 123

1	如今	*rú jīn* now
	滄海桑田	*tsāng hǎi sāng tyán* the vast ocean changed into a mulberry field (i.e., great changes have taken place in the course of time.)
2	滿懷	*mǎnhwái* a lot of (lit., a whole bosom of)
	一把	*yíbǎ* a handful
	荒煙	*hwāngyān* wild smoke
3	迷羊	*míyáng* stray lamb
4	灰沙	*hwēishā* dust and sand
	蔚藍	*wèilán* azure blue (sky)
5	雲峯	*yúnfēng* cloudy peaks
6	仙鄉	*syānsyāng* fairy land

NOTES

預 言 Yùyán

何其芳   *Hé Chí-fāng* (1912 -) Poet and essayist. Born in Szechwan, where he remained with his family until he was fifteen, receiving a strict classical education. In 1931 he entered the National University of Peking to study philosophy. His first book 畫夢錄 *Huà Mèng Lù* won the 大公報 *Dà Gūng Bàu* literary prize as the best essays of 1936. In the same year appeared his first collection of poems in the 漢園集 *Hànywán Jí*. During the Sino-Japanese War, he went to Chengtu, then to Yenan, where he taught in the Lu Hsün Institute of Arts founded in honor of 魯迅 *Lǔ Syùn*. He was in charge of the Yenan Branch of the National Writers' Anti-Aggression Association and edited the Association's publication 大衆文藝 *Dàjùng Wényì*. He is now vice director of the Literary Research Institute of Peking University, and one of the leading critics in Communist China.

page 124

	預言	*yùyán* prophecy ; to prophesy
1	心跳	*syīn tyàu* to palpitate (fearful, apprehensive)
3	私語	*sžyǔ* to whisper
4	麋鹿	*mílù* deer
	馳過	*chŕgwò* to pass quickly
	苔徑	*tái jìng* mossy path
	蹄聲	*tíshēng* sound of the hoofs (蹏 is used interchangeably with 蹄.)
7	温郁	*wēnyù* to be warm and genial

10	癡戀	*chīlyàn*	to be madly in love, dote on
	綠楊	*lyùyáng*	green willow tree
11	合眼	*hé yǎn*	to close eyes
12	温馨	*wēnsyīng*	balmy fragrance

page 125

1	奔波	*bēnbwō*	restless traveling
5	沉鬱	*chényù*	to be low and despondent
	高揚	*gāuyáng*	to be rising and exalted
8	斑文	*bānwén*	stripes, mottled lines
9	籐	*téng*	general name for climbing plants ; rattan
	蟒蛇	*mǎng shé*	python and snake
	交纏	*jyāuchán*	to entwine
10	漏	*lòu*	to fall down, leak out
12	空寥	*kūnglyáu*	to be hollow and desolate

page 126

3	忘倦	*wàng jywàn*	to forget fatigue
5	濃黑	*núng hēi*	heavy darkness
	遮斷	*jēdwàn*	to cover ; to block from view
6	不轉眼地	*bùjwǎnyǎnde*	without turning the eye ; fixedly
7	激動	*jīdùng*	to stir up ; arouse the emotions
8	顫抖	*chàndǒu*	to tremble
9	靜穆	*jìngmù*	to be calm and serene
10	驕傲	*jyāuàu*	to be proud

NOTES

太　陽　*Tàiyang*

艾青　　　*Ài Chīng* (1910 -) Pen name of 蔣海澄 *Jyǎng Hǎi-chéng*. Poet. Born in Chekiang. After graduating from middle school, he studied medicine for a while, but later went to France against his parents' wishes, earning his living by designing figures for porcelain. Shortly after his return to China in 1932, he was arrested for "harboring dangerous thoughts" and was not released until October 1935. Thereafter he became a professional writer, often teaching and nearly always editing magazines. Later he journeyed to Yenan and taught occasionally at Lu Hsün Institute of Arts. He is one of the great living Chinese poets, with an extraordinary capacity for putting the Chinese scene on paper.

page 127

1　　墓塋　　　*mùyíng* graves

3　　死亡之流　*sžwáng jr̄ lyóu* the stream of mortality

4　　山脈　　　*shānmài* mountain range

5　　火輪　　　*hwǒlwún* flaming wheel

　　　飛旋　　　*fēisywán* to whirl around

　　　沙丘　　　*shāchyōu* sandy hill

7　　遮掩　　　*jēyǎn* to conceal

　　　光芒　　　*gwāngmáng* bright rays of the sun, flash of light

8　　呼吸　　　*hūsyī* to breathe

9　　繁枝　　　*fánjr̄* thick twigs

page 128

2	蟄	*jŕ*	to hibernate
	蟲蛹	*chúngyūng*	insects and pupas
5	電力	*dyànlì*	electricity
	召喚	*jàuhwàn*	to call, summon
7	火焰	*hwŏyán*	flame
	撕開	*sz̄kāi*	to tear apart
8	陳腐	*chénfŭ*	to be stale and corrupt
9	擱棄	*gēchì*	to be cast aside, abandoned
	河畔	*hé pàn*	river bank
10	再生	*dzàishēng*	rebirth
	確信	*chywèsyìn*	conviction

當牠來時，我聽見

冬蟄的蟲蛹轉動於地下 1

羣衆在廣場上高聲說話 2

城市從遠方 3

用電力與鋼鐵召喚牠 4

於是我的心胸 5

被火熖之手撕開 6

陳腐的靈魂 7

擱棄在河畔 8

我乃有對於人類再生之確信 9

　　　　　　　　　　10

柳無忌
李田意 合編

現代中國文學讀本

第一冊 戲劇與詩歌

現代中國文學讀本

第一冊 戲劇與詩歌

出版者 耶魯大學遠東出版社

編者 柳無忌 李田意

增訂版
出版日期 一九七五年十月

目錄

第一部

戯劇

壓迫

丁西林

劇中人物：

男客人
女客人
房東太太
老媽子
巡警

佈景：

一間中國舊式的房子。後面一門通院子，左右壁各一門通耳房。房的中間偏右方，一張方桌，四圍幾張小椅。桌上鋪了白布，中間放着一架煤油燈及茶具。偏左方，一張茶几，兩張椅子，靠壁放着。一張椅背上放着一件雨衣，旁邊放着一個手提的皮包。後面的左邊靠牆放着一張類似洗臉架帶有鏡子的小桌，上面放着

11 10 9 8 7 6 5 4 3 2 1

一個時鐘及花瓶。屋內尚有其他的陳設，壁上還有一些字畫，但都很簡單而儉樸。

開幕時，一著粗呢洋服，長筒皮靴的男人坐在茶几旁邊的一張椅上抽煙斗，一個老媽子立在門外，將手伸到屋簷的外邊去試驗有無雨點。

老媽　（走進屋來）雨倒不下了，怎樣還不回來？（從桌上拿了茶壺，走到茶几邊代客人倒茶）

男客　吃東西也得等太太回來？

老媽　（嘆了一口氣）是的，吃東西得等太太回來，房子的事情，也得等太太回來。

男客　好吧，等太太回來吧。橫豎是那麼一回事，太太回來也是那樣，太太不回來也是

那樣。（復坐下）

老媽　（搖頭）看那樣子，太太不像肯答應把這房子租給你。

男客　不把這房子租給我？誰教她受我的定錢？

老媽　是的，那衹怪小姐不好。其實──唉──太太的脾氣也太古怪了。像你先生這樣

的人，有甚麼要緊？深更半夜，房裏有一個男人，還可以有個照應。

男客　這房子以前有人租過沒有？

男客　（不耐煩，站起）唉，你先弄一點東西來吃，好不好？

老媽　東西倒有在那裏，不過這也得等太太回來。

男客　吃東西也得等太太回來？

|16|15|14|13|12|11|10|9|8|7|6|5|4|3|2|1|

老媽　這房子已經空了有一年多了，也沒有租出去。

男客　這房子並不壞，為甚麼沒有人要？

老媽　沒有人要？誰看了都說這房子好，都願意租。這房子又乾淨，又顯亮，前面還有那樣的一個花園。

男客　這樣說為甚麼一年多沒有租出去呢？

老媽　你先生也不是外人，告訴你也沒有甚麼要緊。你知道，我們的太太愛的就是打牌，一天到晚在外邊。家裏就祇有我和小姐兩個人。有人來看房，都是小姐去招呼。有家眷的人，一提到太太，小孩，小姐就把他回了。沒有家眷的人，小姐才答應。等到太太回來，一打聽，說是沒有家眷，太太就把他回了。這樣不要說是一年，就是十年，我看這房子也租不出。

男客　怎麼，像這一回的事，我看以前已經有過麼？

老媽　也不知有過多少次。每回租房，小姐都要和太太吵一次。不過平常小姐不敢做主，這一次她做主受了你先生的定錢，所以才生出這樣的事來。

男客　她如果早做主，這房子老早就租了出去。

老媽　是的，不過平常租房的人，聽說房子不能租給他們，他們也就沒有話說，不像你先生這樣的……

16　15　14　13　12　11　10　9　8　7　6　5　4　3　2　1

男客　古怪，是不是？是的，你們太太的脾氣太古怪了，我的脾氣也太古怪了，這一回
　　　兩個古怪碰在一塊兒，所以這事就不好辦了。不過我也覺得這房子不壞，尤其是
　　　前面的那個小花園。

老媽　看你先生的樣子，一定也是愛清靜的。這裏一天到晚聽不到一點嘈雜的聲音，離
　　　你先生辦事的地方又近，所以……我曾在那裏替你先生想……

男客　你替我想甚麼？

老媽　……就說你先生是有家眷的，家眷要過幾天才來，這樣一說，太太一定可以答應
　　　把這房子租給你。

男客　好了，如果過幾天沒有家眷來，怎樣？

老媽　住了些時，太太看了你先生甚麼都好，她也就不管了。

男客　不行不行，一個人沒有結婚，並沒有犯罪，爲甚麼連房子都租不得？

老媽　啊，我不過覺得你先生這樣的愛這房子，如果租不成功，心裏一定不舒服，所以
　　　那麼瞎想罷了，我原是不懂事的。——啊，這大概是太太回來了。（走到門口高
　　　聲）是太太麼？（外邊答應着）是的，在這兒。（走出。客人也站了起來。少停，
　　　房東太太由後門走進，老媽跟在她的後面）

房東　對不住，勞你等了。

16　15　14　13　12　11　10　9　8　7　6　5　4　3　2　1

男客　我對你不住，打擾了你。我教你們的老媽子不要去驚動你，她沒有聽我的話。

房東　那沒有甚麼。（從一個皮夾子裏拿了一張票子）啊，這是你先生留下的定錢，請你收起來。

男客　啊，對不住，我今天是到這邊來住宿的，不是來討定錢的。

房東　怎麼？昨天我不是對你說明白了麼，說這房子不能租給你？

男客　啊，是的，你說的很明白。

房東　那麼今天你還教人把行李送到這兒來是甚麼意思？

男客　（高興得很）因為教我不要來是你說的，不是我說的，我並沒有答應你說不來，我答應了沒有？

房東　（漸漸的感到不快）你這話我真不大明白，你的意思，好像是說這房子的租不租要由你答應，是不是？

男客　啊，不是，這房子的租不租，自然是要由你答應。不過，既把房子租了給我，這房子的退不退，就得由我答應。你知道，現在這房子不是租不租的問題，是退不退的問題。

房東　（漸漸生起氣來）我這房子是幾時租給你的？

男客　你既受了我的定錢，這房子就算租了給我。

16　15　14　13　12　11　10　9　8　7　6　5　4　3　2　1

房東　真是碰到鬼！我幾時受你的定錢？那是我的女兒，她不懂事。

男客　不懂事？她又不是一個小孩子。

房東　啊，現在這些廢話都不必講。如果你先生有家眷來住，我這房子並不是不租，我是要租一個有家眷的人，我這房子租給你，我沒有話說。

男客　你這話說的毫無道理。你租房的時候，說明了要家眷沒有？我騙了你沒有？

房東　（改用和平的方法）租房的時候沒有說，可是我昨天已經對你先生說過，我們家沒有一個男人……

男客　（停止她）唉，唉，我問你，你租房的時候，你家裏有男人沒有？為甚麼現在才想到？

房東　你這人一點道理不講，我沒有這許多工夫來和你爭論。

老媽　（想做和事老）太太，今天時候也不早，天又下雨，現在要這位先生另外找房子，也不大方便。可不可以讓這位先生暫時在這兒住一宵，明天再想旁的法子。

男客　（固執）不行！這話不是這樣講，如果我不租這房子，我即刻就走，既是受了我的定錢，這房子就非租給我不可！

房東　那麼我告訴你，你今晚非走不可！

男客　（冷笑了一聲）哼！（坐了下來）

房東　（站到他的面前）你走不走？

男客　不走！

房東　王媽，去把巡警叫來。

老媽　啊，太太。

房東　你去叫巡警來。

老媽　巡警來了又怎樣？巡警也得講理呀。

男客　太太，我想……

房東　我教你去叫巡警去，你聽見了沒有？——你去不去？

老媽　好吧。（由後門走出）

房東　要他即刻就來！（由後門走出，用力將門一關。）

男客　（沒有了辦法。袋裏摸出煙包和煙斗，包裏的煙又完了。從皮包裏取出一個煙罐，開了一罐新煙，先把煙包裝滿了，然後裝了煙斗。正想抽煙的時候，忽然來了敲門的聲音。厲聲的）進來！（仍然背了門立着）

女客　（推開門，輕輕走進。身上著了一件雨衣，一手提了一隻小皮包，一手拿了一把雨傘。一進門就開了口，一開了口就有不能停止的勢子）啊，對不起，請你原諒。（男客人急轉過身來，這時他才看見進來的是這樣的一個人）這是很無禮

16　15　14　13　12　11　10　9　8　7　6　5　4　3　2　1

的，我知道，但是我沒有辦法。你們的大門沒有關，我一連敲了好幾下，都沒有人答應，所以祇好一直走進來。

男客　（氣還未平，但沒有忘記把啣在嘴裏的煙斗拿下來放在桌上）你有什麼事？

女客　我？我是到這邊大成公司做事來的，今天剛從北平來。下午五點的車子，直到六點半鐘才到，九十里路，走了兩個半鐘頭，你看！現在我要找一個住宿的地方，在火車站上，我打聽了好幾個地址，一連走了三四家，都沒有找到一間合用的房子。有人告訴我，說這邊還有幾間空房……

男客　（遇到了對頭）啊，你是來租房的！

女客　是的。不知道這邊的房子租出去了沒有？

男客　（狠心的回答）你的運氣不好，這房子剛剛租出去。

女客　啊，你說我運氣不好，我的運氣可真不好。碰到這樣的天氣，這鄉下的路又不好走。你看，我一身的衣服都打濕了。兩隻腳走得發酸。（嘆了一口氣）唉，我可以借你們的凳子坐了歇一回麼？

男客　對不起，請坐。（氣全沒有了）

女客　（放下皮包雨傘）謝謝你。（坐在茶几裏邊的一張椅上，向四邊觀察房裏的一切）

男客　（引起了趣味。坐在方桌旁的一張小椅上）剛才你說你是到大成公司來做事的，

女客　不知道在那邊担任的甚麼事？——啊，也許我不應該問。

　　　不應該問？那有甚麼！這又不是不可以告訴人的事。前兩個星期，他們在報上登

　　　了一個廣告，要聘請一位書記。那個廣告，甚麼報上都有，我想你一定看到的。

男客　（點了一點頭）

女客　上星期五，他們又在報上登了一個啟事，說『敝公司擬聘書記一席，現已聘定，

　　　所有親友寄來薦書，恕不一一作覆，特此聲明。』這個啟事，你看見了沒有？

男客　（又點了一點頭）

女客　那位聘定的書記就是我。你沒有想到吧？——你沒有想到是一個女人吧？

男客　這倒沒有想到。

女客　（得意得很）不過現在要怎樣辦呢？你替我想想，後天就要到公司裏去接事，現

　　　在連住的地方還沒有找到。從六點半鐘一直走到現在，就沒有停腳。不瞞你說，

　　　我連飯還沒有吃呢。（起身整理了一回衣，走到鏡子的前面照臉）

男客　（好像很同情的樣子）飯還沒有吃？那怎麼行？這一層說不定我或者可以幫助

　　　你。（起身倒了一杯茶）

女客　謝謝你，我不過是告訴你。我不是來騙飯吃的。

男客　啊，對不起！——好，請先喝一杯茶吧。

女客　謝謝。（復坐原處）

男客　（袋裏摸出紙煙盒）你不抽煙？

女客　我不抽煙，不過我並不反對旁人抽煙。（喝了一口茶）

男客　謝謝你。（放回煙盒，收了煙斗，背轉了身，燃火抽煙）

女客　（摸到她的腳）天呀！你看我的這雙腳，還像是人的腳麼……

男客　（急轉過身來）怎麼樣？

女客　不僅是水，連泥都走進去了！

男客　（殷勤起來）那眞糟。要不要換襪子？如果要換襪子，我可以走到外邊去。

女客　謝謝你，我不要換襪子。就是換襪子，也用不着把你趕到外邊去。

男客　不要緊，如果襪子沒有帶，我還可以借你一雙。

女客　謝謝你，你的好意我很感激，不過換牠有甚麼用處？反正是要到水裏走去的。

男客　要到水裏走去？——幹麼要到水裏走去？

女客　不到水裏走去有甚麼辦法？這樣漆黑的天，一到街上，你還分得出那裏是水那裏是路來麼？

男客　（如有所思）

女客　（又喝了一口茶，嘆了一口氣，起身告辭）啊，打擾了你，對不住得很。（拿了

皮包雨傘，預備走出）

男客　（阻止她）不用忙，再歇一回兒。——剛才你說，你是要租房的，是不是？

女客　（面向了他）怎麼，我說了半天，你還沒有聽懂麼？

男客　聽是聽懂了。不過……唉，你看這三間房子怎麼樣？

女客　怎麼，你不是說已經租出去了麼？（放下皮包）

男客　租是租出去了，不過也許可以讓給你。

女客　（高興起來）可以讓給我？真的麼？（放下雨傘）

男客　自然是真的。（又替她倒好了一杯茶）

女客　（坐下，接了茶）謝謝。不過為甚麼可以讓給我？是不是這房子如果我願租，你就可以不租給那個人？

男客　（搖頭）

女客　不然，你剛才說的是句謊話，這房子就沒有租出去？

男客　不，我說的是實話。這房子已經租出去了。現在也不是不租給那個人。我說可以讓給你，是說已經租好這房的那個人，自己願意讓給你。

女客　那我可不明白。為甚麼那個人願意把房子讓給我？他連見都沒有見過我，為甚麼要把房子讓給我？

男客　那你不用管。

女客　這房子鬧鬼不鬧鬼？

男客　怎麼，難道你怕鬼麼？

女客　啊，我是不怕鬼的，我說也許那個人怕鬼。

男客　啊，那個人也是不怕鬼的。——不管有鬼沒有鬼，讓我們來看看房子，好不好？（從桌下拿了燈引她看房。）這是一間睡房。（開了右壁的門，讓她走進）蘆葦的頂篷，洋灰地，洋式床，現成的鋪蓋。窗子外面是一個小小的花園。一清早就可聽到鳥的聲音。白天撩開窗簾，滿屋裏都是太陽。（女客人走出。又把她引到左邊的耳房）這邊也是一個睡房。鋪蓋傢具也是現成的。房間的大小，和那邊一樣。　就是光線差一點。一個人住的時候，這裏可以做睡房，那邊可以做書房。（女客人走出）中間可以吃飯會客。（放下燈）這屋子又乾淨，又顯亮，一天到晚，聽不到一點嘈雜的聲音。這裏離你辦事的地方又近。我看這房子於你再合式沒有了。

女客　這三間房子租多少錢？（坐下）

男客　啊，便宜得很。這樣的三間房子，只租五塊錢一月。

女客　房子倒不錯，房價也不貴。（想了一想）這房子真的可以讓給我嗎？

男客　　自然是眞的，爲什麼要騙你？

女客　　不過今晚就來住，總不行吧？

男客　　行，行。（好像忽然想起一件事來）不過——你結了婚沒有？

女客　　（跳了起來，挺了胸脯，竪起眉毛）甚麼！

男客　　（還要補一句）你結了婚沒有？

女客　　（怒了）你這話問的太無道理？

男客　　太無道理？

女客　　簡直是一種侮辱！

男客　　（高興起來）「侮辱」，對了，一點都不錯，我也是這樣說。但是現在有房出租的人，似乎最重要的是先要知道你結婚沒有。

女客　　我結婚沒有，干你甚麼事？

男客　　是的，一點都不錯，我結婚沒有，干她們甚麼事？可是她們一定要問，你說奇怪不奇怪？

女客　　我完全不懂你的意思。

男客　　誰說你懂？你自然不懂我的意思。不過你不要性急，讓我告訴你，你就會懂。

　　——剛才你說，你是到這邊大成公司來做事的，是不是？……

女客　你這人的記憶力眞壞，怎麼剛說過了的話，即刻就忘了。　　　　　　　　　1

男客　不要生氣。我不過是告訴你，我也是到這邊大成公司來做事的。　　　　　　2

女客　你也是到大成來做事的？　　　　　　　　　　　　　　　　　　　　　　　3

男客　是的。你沒有想到吧？　　　　　　　　　　　　　　　　　　　　　　　　4

女客　你在大成做甚麼事？　　　　　　　　　　　　　　　　　　　　　　　　　5

男客　我在這邊當工程師。　　　　　　　　　　　　　　　　　　　　　　　　　6

女客　這樣說，你並不是這裏的房東？　　　　　　　　　　　　　　　　　　　　7

男客　誰說我是這裏的房東？我說了我是這裏的房東沒有？你看我樣子，像一個房東　8

　　　廢？　　　　　　　　　　　　　　　　　　　　　　　　　　　　　　　　9

女客　（搶着說）啊，我知道了！你是這裏的房客！這三間房子是你租的，現在你覺得　10

　　　不合式，想把牠退了。　　　　　　　　　　　　　　　　　　　　　　　　11

男客　想把牠退了！誰說把牠退了？　　　　　　　　　　　　　　　　　　　　　12

女客　剛才你不是說這房子可以讓給我的麼？　　　　　　　　　　　　　　　　　13

男客　是的，我是說可以讓，沒有說要退。　　　　　　　　　　　　　　　　　　14

女客　那我更加不明白了。你既不想退，爲甚麼要讓呢？　　　　　　　　　　　　15

男客　你眞的不明白麼？　　　　　　　　　　　　　　　　　　　　　　　　　　16

女客　眞的不明白。（坐下）

男客　因爲——我看了你……啊，不是，因爲房東不肯租給我。

女客　爲甚麼房東不肯租給你？

男客　啊，可是這婚姻的問題。現在我們講到題目上來了。一星期以前，我到這裏來看房子，碰到了房東小姐。一見了我，她就盤問我，問我有沒有老太太，有沒有小孩子，有沒有兄弟姊妹，直等到我明明白白地告訴了她我是沒有結過婚，她才滿了意。連房價也沒有多講，她就答應了把房子租給我。

女客　懂麼？她一定知道了你是一個工程師，她想嫁給你！

男客　眞的麼？這我倒沒有想到。——昨天下午，我到這裏來的時候，她們老太太告訴我，說如果我沒有家眷來同住，她這房子不能租給我，你說可惡不可惡？她把這話來要挾我，你說可惡不可惡？

女客　爲什麼沒有家眷來同住，這房子就不能租給你？

男客　我不知道啊。她說她們家裏沒有男人。

女客　笑話。

男客　這簡直是一種侮辱，是不是？

女客　是的。——後來怎麼樣？

16　15　14　13　12　11　10　9　8　7　6　5　4　3　2　1

男客　　後來我把她教訓了一頓。　　　　　　　　　　　　　　　　　1

女客　　她明白了這個道理沒有？　　　　　　　　　　　　　　　　2

男客　　明白了這個道理？一個人一過了四十歲，他腦子裏就已經裝滿了舊的道理，再也　　3

　　　　沒有地方裝新的道理，我告訴你。　　　　　　　　　　　　4

女客　　現在怎麼樣？　　　　　　　　　　　　　　　　　　　　　5

男客　　現在？現在我不走！　　　　　　　　　　　　　　　　　　6

女客　　她呢？　　　　　　　　　　　　　　　　　　　　　　　　7

男客　　她？她去叫巡警。　　　　　　　　　　　　　　　　　　　8

女客　　叫巡警？叫巡警來幹甚麼？　　　　　　　　　　　　　　　9

男客　　叫巡警來攆我！　　　　　　　　　　　　　　　　　　　　10

女客　　眞的麼！　　　　　　　　　　　　　　　　　　　　　　　11

男客　　爲甚麼要騙你？你如果不相信，等一回兒巡警就要來，你自己看好了。　　12

女客　　這倒是怪有趣的事。不過巡警如果眞的要攆你，你怎麼樣？　　13

男客　　你沒有來以前，我不知道怎樣。現在我有了主意。　　　　14

女客　　你預備怎樣？　　　　　　　　　　　　　　　　　　　　　15

男客　　我把巡警痛打一頓，讓他把我帶到巡警局裏去，敎房東把房子租給你。這樣一　　16

女客　來，我們兩個人就都有住宿的地方。

女客　那不行（若有所思）。

男客　那為甚麼不行？

女客　你還是沒有出那口氣。——唉，我倒有個主意。

男客　你有甚麼主意？

女客　（少頓）讓我來做你的太太，好不好？

男客　甚麼！

女客　啊，你不用嚇得那麼樣。我不是向你求婚。

男客　啊，你誤會了我的意思，——我——我——因為我實在沒有想到這個方法。

女客　這是最妙的一個方法，她說你沒有家眷同住，這房子就不能租給你。現在你說你有了家眷，看她有甚麼話說？

男客　她一定沒有話說。不過——你願意麼？

女客　我為甚麼不願意？這於我有甚麼損害？——又不是真的做你的太太。

男客　啊，謝謝你！

女客　你不要把我的意思弄錯。我不是說做了你的太太，我就有甚麼損害，那完全是另外一個問題。

男客　是的，那完全是另外一個問題。不過你寫我把租房的這個問題解決了，我總應該
　　　向你道謝。

女客　噓！道謝？（側耳靜聽）

男客　不錯，不錯。

女客　我聽見有人說話。

男客　那一定是巡警！（急促的）唉，不過我已經說過我是沒有家眷的，現在怎麼對她
　　　們講？

女客　就說我們吵了嘴，你是逃出來的，不願意給人知道……

男客　（巡警已經走到門外，急忙的點了一點頭，教她不要再講話）吁！（男客人坐在
　　　方桌邊，裝作生氣的樣子。女客人坐在茶几旁邊。後門由外推開，走進一個巡
　　　警，手裏提了一個風燈，後面跟了老媽和房東太太。她們看見房裏來了一個女
　　　人，非常驚訝。房裏來的這個女人，見她們來了，起了一回身，向她們行了一個
　　　很謙和的禮。巡警將風燈放在桌上，與那位生氣的先生行了一禮）

巡警　您貴姓？

男客　（不客氣的）我姓吳。

巡警　（把頭點了一點）啊。——府上是？

16　15　14　13　12　11　10　9　8　7　6　5　4　3　2　1

男客　府上？我沒有府上。

女客　（開始做起受了委曲的太太來）啊，你是拿定主意不要家了，是不是？

巡警　（注意到插嘴的人，向男客人）這位……貴姓是？

男客　（答不出，看了女客一眼，女客也正在代他為難。他祇好開始做起依舊睹氣的丈夫來）我不知道。你問她自己好了。

巡警　（真的問她自己）您貴姓？

女客　（很高興的）我？我——也姓吳。

巡警　啊，您也姓吳。

女客　是的。

巡警　（再也想不出別的話）府上是？

女客　我？我住在北平西四牌樓太平胡同關帝廟對面，門牌三百七十五號，電話西局四千六百九十二——啊，你把牠寫下來吧，等一回兒你一定要忘記。

巡警　（真的摸出一本小簿子來）北平……（寫字）

女客　西四牌樓太平胡同，（讓巡警寫）關帝廟對面。

巡警　門牌多少？

女客　三百七十五號。電話西局——四千——六百——九十二。

巡警　（寫完了）謝謝您。（藏好了簿子，又轉到男客）您是來這邊租房的，是不是？

男客　不是！我是來這邊住宿的，這房子我老早就租了。

巡警　（難住了。沒有了辦法，又轉到女客）您是來這邊？……

女客　我？我是來這邊找人的。

房東　（不能再耐了）你到這邊來找人？

女客　（很客氣的向她點了一點頭）我到這邊來找我的男人。

房東　找你的男人？誰是你的男人？

女客　我想你應該知道吧！――你既把房子都租了給他。

房東　怎麼！這位先生是你的男人麼？

女客　我不知道。你問他好了，看他承認不承認？

老媽　（也不能再耐了）太太，你看怎麼樣！我老早就對您說過，這位先生一定是有太太的，您不信。

巡警　（糊塗了）怎麼？剛才你們不是說這位先生沒有家眷，怎麼現在他又有了家眷？

老媽　不要糊塗吧。剛才這位太太還沒來，我們怎麼會知道？如果這位太太早來這裏，還可以省了我在雨地裏走一趟呢。

女客　對你不住。這實在不能怪我，五點鐘的車子，六點半鐘才到這裏。

16　15　14　13　12　11　10　9　8　7　6　5　4　3　2　1

老媽　請您不要多心，我不過是說他太不懂事。

巡警　這話可得要說明白了。太太要我到這邊來，是說這位先生租了這三間房子，要一個人在這邊住。這屋裏住的都是堂客，他先生一個人在這裏住，很不方便，是那麼個意思。現在這位先生的太太既是來了，這事就好辦。如果太太是和先生在這邊同住，那就沒有我的事，如果太太不在這邊住，這件事還得……

老媽　不要瞎說吧。太太自然是在這邊住。——一看還不知道——先生和太太不在這邊住，太太不過是爲了一點小事，鬧了一點意見，你不來勸解勸解，還來說那樣的話。太太不在這邊住，到那裏住去？——好了，現在沒有你的事了，你趕緊回去打你的牌去吧，

巡警　（把風燈送到他手裏）走！走！

女客　這樣說，那就沒有我的事了。好了，再見，再見。

巡警　再見。你放心好了，哪一天我不在這裏住的時候，我通知你就是了。

女客　對不起，打擾，打擾。（巡警走出。老媽興高采烈的拿了茶壺走出。房東太太承認了失敗，看了她的客人一眼，也祇好板了面孔走出。）

男客　（關上門，想起了一個老早就應該問而還沒有問的問題，忽然轉過頭來）啊，你姓甚麼？

女客　我——啊——我……（幕下）

16　15　14　13　12　11　10　9　8　7　6　5　4　3　2　1

藝術家

熊佛西

劇中人物：

 林可梅   1

 其妻   2

 其弟   3

 買掌櫃   4

佈景：

 林可梅的畫室，遍壁掛的是林的作品。開幕時林正在畫畫，其妻很不高興的 5

 由裏面出來。   6

妻　十二點鐘已經敲過了，你知道嗎？ 7

林　我知道。   8

妻　米又完了，你知道嗎？ 9

           10

           11

林　我知道。

妻　油鹽亦沒了，你知道嗎？

林　我知道。

妻　今天又要付房錢，你知道嗎？

林　我知道。

妻　我媽今天五十歲，你知道嗎？

林　我知道。

妻　你都知道？你都知道什麼？

林　我知道。

妻　哈哈！

林　「哈哈？」哈哈什麼！

妻　你瞧，太太，你瞧我這兩筆畫多麼有趣呀！

林　我和你說的話，你聽見了麼？

妻　聽見了！聽見了！

林　你聽見我說了些什麼？

妻　你說！

林　⋯⋯⋯⋯⋯

16　15　14　13　12　11　10　9　8　7　6　5　4　3　2　1

林　你說這張畫是我的傑作！

妻　胡說！

林　是的！是的！我想起來了！是的，你剛才說你要我替你畫一張像！好極了，好極
了！請你坐下，我替你速寫一張！自從咱們結婚到現在，我從來沒替你畫過像。今
天是頂好的機會！來，請坐下，（扶着其妻坐下）請別動！請別動！唉！請你別動，

妻　別動，你偏要動！

林　我要動！我偏要動！我存心要動！

妻　那麼我只好不畫？

林　誰教你自討沒趣！

妻　（林繼續畫他原來的畫。）

林　我和你說的話，你到底聽見了沒有？

妻　沒聽見，勞你駕，請再說一遍！

林　十二點鐘已經敲過了！

妻　調午飯！

林　米又完了！

妻　買去！

　　16　15　14　13　12　11　10　9　8　7　6　5　4　3　2　1

妻　油鹽亦沒了！

林　買去！

妻　今天又要付房錢！

林　付去！

妻　我媽今天五十歲！

林　買禮物拜壽去！

妻　拿錢來！

林　錢？

妻　錢！

林　十號不是給了你五塊錢麼？

妻　今天幾號了，你知道麼？

林　今天？

妻　我勸你少做點夢罷？十號交我五塊錢，用到今天十七號，足足用了七天，你還不滿足嗎？你還以為我浪費了一文半文嗎？

林　好了，好了，求你別鬧了，讓我畫完這張傑作再說！

妻　你現在不交錢來，你想畫畫，是辦不到的！

林　那麼你要怎樣？　　　　　　　　　　　　　　　　　　1

妻　我不要怎樣！我只要錢！　　　　　　　　　　　　　2

林　請你等一等！　　　　　　　　　　　　　　　　　　3

妻　多久？　　　　　　　　　　　　　　　　　　　　　4

林　半點鐘，我已經差弟弟賣畫去了。　　　　　　　　　5

妻　你想你的畫能賣錢嗎？　　　　　　　　　　　　　　6

林　弟弟拿去賣的兩張畫，是我最得意的作品，我想至少應該賣一千塊錢。假如賣了一　　7

　　千塊錢，不但咱們的油鹽柴米都有了，就是你天天鬧着的金剛鑽，亦可以到手了。　8

　　從此我亦可以安心畫幾天畫了！　　　　　　　　　　9

妻　我算活到霉，嫁給你這樣一個窮鬼！　　　　　　　10

林　我看這是你的福氣，嫁了像我這樣的一個藝術家！　11

妻　我的福氣？哼！藝術家！我聽到都肉麻了，假如我沒有嫁你，我的摩托車早已坐上　12

　　了！　　　　　　　　　　　　　　　　　　　　　13

林　也許。　　　　　　　　　　　　　　　　　　　　14

妻　金鋼鑽早已戴上了！　　　　　　　　　　　　　　15

林　也許。　　　　　　　　　　　　　　　　　　　　16

妻　高大的洋樓早已住上了！　　　　　　　　　　　　　　　　　　1

林　也許。　　　　　　　　　　　　　　　　　　　　　　　　　　2

妻　綢的緞的早已穿上了！　　　　　　　　　　　　　　　　　　　3

林　也許。　　　　　　　　　　　　　　　　　　　　　　　　　　4

妻　「也許？」「也許」什麼？「也許」就是嫁壞了你這個倒霉鬼！　5

林　也許。　　　　　　　　　　　　　　　　　　　　　　　　　　6

妻　「也許？」「也許」什麼？　　　　　　　　　　　　　　　　　7

林　你還在「也許？」我不准你再「也許」了！　　　　　　　　　　8

（將林手中的畫筆奪下。）

妻　我的太太，請你不要鬧了，好不好？　　　　　　　　　　　　9

林　你喊我太太也不成！　　　　　　　　　　　　　　　　　　　10

妻　我的老太太！　　　　　　　　　　　　　　　　　　　　　　11

林　你叫我是你家裏十八代的老祖宗也不成！　　　　　　　　　　12

妻　那麼你要怎樣？　　　　　　　　　　　　　　　　　　　　　13

林　我不要怎樣！我只討厭你再畫畫！畫畫的都是些窮鬼！　　　　14

妻　不願你躲在家裏鬼畫！我要你從現在起發誓不再畫畫！我情願你每天出去拉洋車，　15

林　什麼！你要我起誓，從此不畫畫？　　　　　　　　　　　　　16

妻　對！

林　無論你叫我幹嗎都成，祇是禁止我畫畫，絕對不成！

妻　（抓住林的領口）成不成？

林　不成！

妻　（揙住他的耳朵）成不成？

林　也不成！

妻　成不成！

林　你把我的耳朵箝掉了，還是不成！

妻　那麼要怎樣才成？

林　除非你先抬棺材來！

（妻狠狠的揙了一下才鬆手。）

妻　我至終不懂你為什麼捨不得你這幾筆——「寶貝畫！」

林　就是因為它是我的寶貝，我才捨不得拋棄它。

妻　你這畫的是什麼？

林　是我的傑作。

妻　這好像畫的是個窮鬼。

16　15　14　13　12　11　10　9　8　7　6　5　4　3　2　1

林　這就是我理想的藝術家！

妻　對了，這活像一個窮鬼！

林　窮鬼並沒有什麼可怕。

林　你不怕窮麼？

妻　怕窮不畫畫！

林　你不怕餓麼？

妻　怕餓不畫畫！

林　那麼你怕什麼？

妻　只怕你！

林　只怕我？

妻　只怕你——不准我畫畫！

林　只要你的畫能賣錢，我又不是瘋了，爲什麼不讓你畫呢？

妻　你讓我畫？

林　只要你有錢！

妻　只要你有錢！

林　那麼請你把畫筆交還我？

妻　請你先拿錢來。

16　15　14　13　12　11　10　9　8　7　6　5　4　3　2　1

林　弟弟回來就有錢。弟弟回來了！錢來了！錢來了！

（林的弟弟可松上。）

林　怎麼樣，弟弟？

弟　好極了，人人都說你是中國現代第一流的畫家。

妻　真的？

弟　真的，凡看過他的畫的，都說他有創造的天才！

妻　真的？

弟　真的！那個古玩舖裏的賈掌櫃說：你的畫是前無古人，後無來者；說中國的畫風，到你手上是一大轉機；說你的畫的妙處是打破了中國畫一切傳統的思想，獨闢天地，很有革命的精神！

妻　真的？

弟　自然。我拿給學校裏的同事看了，他們都是異口同聲的稱讚，所以他們千拜託，萬拜託，請我轉託你畫幾張送給他們。

妻　我倒沒想到一般人會這樣的歡喜你的畫。

林　哈哈！你沒有想到罷？

妻　倒瞧你不出！

1　2　3　4　5　6　7　8　9　10　11　12　13　14　15　16

林　你就從來沒有瞧過我！

妻　弟弟，他的畫既然這樣受人歡迎，可以賣多少錢一張？

弟　在某種條件之下，可以賣五千塊錢一張！

妻　多少？

弟　五千！

妻　多少？

弟　五千！

妻　五千？

弟　五千！

妻　五千？

弟　五千！

妻　誰說的？

弟　古玩舖裏的買掌櫃。

妻　如此說來，我們豈不要馬上發財嗎？

弟　可不是嗎？嫂嫂天天記念的金鋼鑽和汽車不久就要到手了！

妻　你今天賣了幾張畫？

弟　哥哥只給了我兩張。

妻　賣給誰了。

16　15　14　13　12　11　10　9　8　7　6　5　4　3　2　1

弟　　古玩舖的賈掌櫃。

妻　　錢呢？

弟　　在這兒。

妻　　現洋還是鈔票？

弟　　現洋！

　　（弟由袋內掏出一元現洋給妻。）

妻　　這只是一塊錢？還有九千九百九十九塊呢？

弟　　兩張畫的代價統統在這兒！

妻　　統統在這兒？

弟　　都在這兒！

妻　　你不是說他的畫可以賣五千塊錢一張嗎？現在既是賣了兩張，就應該有一萬塊錢的收入？

弟　　是的；但是在哥哥未死以前，只能賣五毛錢一張！

妻　　我不懂你這話的意思？

弟　　據古玩舖賈掌櫃說：哥哥的畫雖好，可是現在不值錢。一定要等他死了以後，值五毛的可以值五千！

妻　有這麼大的分別麼？

弟　可不是嗎？不管好人壞人，只要他死了，人家就恭維他。你只要跑到祭堂裏去，看

着那些輓聯，便知道「死」的好處。據賈掌櫃說：一切藝術家亦是如此；他們在生

的時候，連飯都沒有吃，他們的作品一錢不值；只要他們一死，便大大值錢了！

妻　既是這樣，那麼請你的哥哥趕快死罷。

弟　這是我們現在發財唯一的方法！

（妻又走過去，將林的畫筆奪下。）

林　我的好太太，請你不要鬧了罷，讓我畫完這張傑作。

妻　就是你畫完了這張傑作，亦是沒有用的。我們剛才說的話，你聽見沒有？

林　沒有。

妻　你的兩張畫，只賣了一圓錢！

林　只賣了一塊錢？

妻　可不是嗎？

林　那麼趕快去替我拿回來，我不賣了！這簡直是侮辱我的人格！這簡直不能活了！

妻　不能活了，你就趕快死去罷。你死了，我們一家子都好了。

林　為什麼？

妻　你死了，你的畫可以賣五千塊錢一張！

林　這話是真的嗎，弟弟？

弟　只要你一死，我們馬上就發財了。你可以死嗎，哥哥？

林　我的傑作還未畫完，我是死不得的。

弟　倘若你不死，你的傑作永遠不會成為傑作！

林　為了我的金鋼鑽，為了我的汽車，你不能不死！

妻　我捨不得這個世界！

林　少說廢話罷！

妻　其實我是捨不得你！假如你願意同我一塊兒死，我就馬上可以死！

林　少肉麻點罷！我這會兒的霉還沒有倒够嗎？還沒有窮怕嗎？還要和你一塊兒去做餓鬼嗎？

弟　我倒有個絕妙的法子：你們倆一個也不必死，照樣可以發財。

妻　什麼法子？

弟　只要哥哥現在躺在地下假裝死了，嫂嫂跪在傍邊很傷心的哭着，我就趕快去告訴古玩舖裏的賈掌櫃說，哥哥得急症死了，叫他趕快來買畫！你們看這個法子好不好？

妻　好極了，這個法子好極了！現在我們馬上假裝起來！你趕快去找賈掌櫃來罷，越快

16　15　14　13　12　11　10　9　8　7　6　5　4　3　2　1

林　越好！

林　慢點，慢點，我看這個法子很不妥當，因為這裏面帶着一點欺騙的色彩。

妻　你又傻起來了！

弟　將畫賣錢，這有什麼欺騙？

林　藝術家有他的人格，我決不能欺騙人！

妻　你少傻點罷。還不乖乖的替我睡下！

林　我不能幹這種不道德的事情！

　　（說話之間，林妻又揑住林的耳朵。）

妻　你睡不睡下裝死？

林　好，好，我睡下！反正我這條命是沒有了！

弟　地下應該墊塊氈子，頭上蓋塊手巾。你們趕快假裝起來罷，我去找買掌櫃。

妻　古玩舖離這兒有多遠？

弟　不遠，一過街就到。

妻　你快去快回。

　　（弟下。妻將氈子鋪地，迫林睡下，用白手巾罩住臉，點了一對殘燭。然後跪下，放聲大哭。）

16　15　14　13　12　11　10　9　8　7　6　5　4　3　2　1

林　你哭什麼？

妻　你死了，我怎能不哭？

林　我沒有死呢！

妻　但是我要當你真死了！

林　倘若我真死了，恐怕你不會哭得這麼傷心？

妻　倘若你真死了，也就用不着我哭！

林　你好狠的心！

妻　誰叫你沒半寸用！

林　你說我沒有用，我不死了！

妻　（林突然爬起來。）

你有用，你的用處大着啦！請你趕快睡下罷！你聽！有人來了！

弟　（林又睡下，其妻放聲大哭。賈掌櫃與林弟上。）

說也奇怪？早晨還在畫畫，不知到這會兒人就死了！唉！真是天有不測風雲，人有旦夕禍福！

賈　這一定是急症，否則決不會死得這麼快？

弟　急症，急症，一點兒不錯！

　　16　15　14　13　12　11　10　9　8　7　6　5　4　3　2　1

買　現在你打算把他的作品統統賣給我？

弟　對。

買　要多少錢？

弟　嫂嫂，請別哭了罷！人死了哭也哭不活的。現在賈掌櫃要包銷哥哥的畫，你看要賣多少錢？

買　多少錢？

妻　像你哥哥這樣一個有天才有名譽的畫家現在死了，我怎能不哭呢？

弟　哭自然要哭，可是不必哭得太厲害！現在賈掌櫃問哥哥的作品究竟要賣多少錢？

妻　非十萬不賣！

買　太多，太多，這幾張畫那能值得十萬？不成，不成！林可梅雖然是現在第一流的畫家，也不能賣這麼高的價錢。

弟　裏面還有呢！大大小小一共一百多張，讓我們一塊兒進去看看！

　　（林弟引着買入內，林又突然爬起來。）

妻　你……你……你趕快睡下罷！

林　你打死我，我再也不睡下了！

妻　爲什麼？

林　你的心太狠了！你要別人十萬塊錢？要這麼些錢幹嗎？要來放在那兒？怎麼用法？

　　16　15　14　13　12　11　10　9　8　7　6　5　4　3　2　1

妻　你少傻點罷,我的爺爺!請你趕快睡下!他們出來了,出來了。你聽!你聽!

買　(妻又逼着林睡下。買與林弟上。)
　　令兄眞是一個有天才的畫家,的確有幾幅不朽的作品!不過十萬塊錢還是太貴一點,可不可以少一點?

弟　少多少呢?

買　八萬成不成?

弟　嫂嫂,八萬成不成?

妻　就算八萬五罷?

買　至少九萬不賣!

妻　可是要現錢。

買　馬上就寫支票。

弟　這好極了。

買　(買寫支票交給林弟。)
　　八萬五。

弟　一點兒不錯。

買　不過我也要請你們寫一張字據,說明令兄的作品,不管大大小小統統已經賣給我

16　15　14　13　12　11　10　9　8　7　6　5　4　3　2　1

弟　了。

這是當然的。讓我就借你的筆寫。

（寫畢交給買。）

買　（念）「立賣字人林可松，今將其兄可梅所有作品賣與立興古玩舖，賣價八萬五千，當面收訖，此據。」

弟　沒有錯罷？

買　沒錯。那麼我現在去找人來幫忙抬畫，回頭見！

弟　回頭見！

（買下。林起來。大家都是笑容滿臉。）

林　現在你們發財了！

妻　發財了！

林　那麼請你們再也不要鬧我了，讓我完成這張傑作！

妻　現在誰也不鬧你了！

（林可梅又擺起畫架來，依舊畫他那張未完的畫。）

妻　弟弟，趕快去叫一輛汽車來！

弟　嫂嫂要上那兒去！

妻　先上銀行兌錢，再去買金鋼鑽，然後再去買汽車。

弟　我可以同嫂嫂一塊兒去麼？

妻　好罷，咱們同去？

弟　哥哥，你不去麼？

（妻與弟同下。片刻，賈掌櫃上。）

賈　奇怪，怎麼這兒的喪事就辦完了麼？

林　喪事？誰的喪事？

賈　林可梅先生的喪事！

林　您貴姓？

賈　我姓賈。

林　您來幹嗎的？

賈　我來取畫的。

林　取畫的？取什麼人的畫？

賈　取林可梅先生的畫。

林　您為什麼要來取他的畫？您與他有什麼關係？

賈　這不是林宅麼？

16　15　14　13　12　11　10　9　8　7　6　5　4　3　2　1

林　是林宅。

賈　林可梅先生不是剛才得急症死了麼？

林　誰說他得急症死了？

賈　我親眼看見他死的！他的畫統統都賣給我了！

林　誰經手賣給你的？

賈　林太太和林先生的弟弟！

林　有什麼憑據？

賈　這不是憑據嗎？

（賈將那張字據交給林可梅看。）

林　對！

賈　你不能承認這張字據？

林　我不能承認這張字據！

賈　你曾見過林可梅本人麼？

林　你是這林府上的什麼人？

賈　我從來沒見過他。但是我們藝術界裏對於他的作品非常欽佩，我個人尤其是喜歡他的東西！可惜他已經歸天了，我不能得着機會拜見他！

16　15　14　13　12　11　10　9　8　7　6　5　4　3　2　1

林　你現在願意見他麼?

買　先生別和我開玩笑龍!先生貴姓?

林　林!

買　台甫?

林　可梅,有名的畫家林可梅就是我!

買　打鬼!打鬼!打鬼!

林　打鬼!打什麼鬼?我剛才並沒死,我剛才是被我的太太逼得沒法纔裝死!

買　裝死?

林　裝死!

買　真的你沒死?

林　人死了,還會站在這兒說話嗎?

買　那麼請你還我的錢!

林　我並沒拿你的錢,請你不要在這兒和我麻煩龍!

(此時林又坐下畫畫,林妻與弟上。)

買　好,你們回來了?好!好極了!咱們一塊兒打官司去!咱們一塊兒打官司去!

妻　為什麼打官司去?

16　15　14　13　12　11　10　9　8　7　6　5　4　3　2　1

買　不願意打官司，就還錢給我！

弟　為什麼還錢給你？

買　咱們用不着多說，反正你們寫有字據在我這兒！

弟　最好請你現在再把那張字據仔細看看，上面究竟怎樣寫的？

買　（念）「立賣字人林可松，今將其兄林可梅所有作品賣與立興古玩鋪，賣價八萬五千，當面收訖。」這不是寫得很清楚嗎？

弟　對，這的確寫得很清楚。現在我哥哥的作品統統都在這兒，你搬去就得了，還有什麼麻煩可搗呢？

買　我現在不要他的作品了！

弟　為什麼？

買　林可梅既是沒死，他的作品就一錢不值了。所以現在只有兩條路：一條是還我八萬五千塊錢；一條是你們把林可梅趕快弄死！不然，咱們就打官司去！

弟　那麼請便罷！

買　那麼，咱們打官司去！

弟　你不要做夢罷！倘去打官司，你更要倒霉！我那字據上，明明寫着將「其」兄林可梅所有作品賣與立興古玩鋪，並沒有寫着「先兄」或「亡兄」！總而言之，賣畫給

16　15　14　13　12　11　10　9　8　7　6　5　4　3　2　1

買　你，可是實事；至於說非要<u>林可梅</u>死的話，從這張字據上找不出這個意義！　1

買　不成！我現在非要他死不可！　2

妻　他不死，你怎樣？　3

買　他不死，我就死！　4

妻　爲什麼要你死呢？　5

買　請你們替我設身處地的想想，我花了八萬五千現洋做這筆生意，實指望從這裏面叨　6

點光；殊不知上了你們這麼大的一個當，就是我不尋死，也會氣死！假如你們現在　7

再能把<u>林可梅</u>弄死，我再給你們三萬塊錢，我也心願；但求你們不要騙我！　8

妻　眞的再給三萬？　9

買　我馬上就寫支票，只要你能把他再弄死一次！其實我並不要他死久，只要他再死一　10

年就够了。　11

弟　我不懂你這話的意思？　12

買　因爲在他死的這一年中間，我就可以把他的畫統統賣完；只要他的畫賣完了，他再　13

死不死，與我就毫不相干！反正這筆生意我沒虧本！　14

妻　你拿支票來？　15

你可以把他弄死嗎？　16

妻　當然！（賈簽票給林妻。）

賈　三萬。現在請你馬上把他弄死！

　　（妻此時又捏住林可梅的耳朵，叫他再睡下。）

林　我的太太，我只要三筆，我的傑作就可以完成了！

妻　我的好丈夫，我要請你再死一次——照原先那樣睡下！

林　我的太太，請你發點慈悲心罷！

妻　倘若你現在不假死，我停會兒就要你眞死！

林　我倒情願眞死！

妻　我倒捨不得你眞死！眞死只有一次，假死可以有無數一次！

林　我不願意欺騙社會！

妻　那麽社會就要欺騙你！

弟　不要麻煩！乾脆死就得了！

　　（妻死命的將林弄倒地下，仍然用白布罩住他的臉。弟幫忙點着蠟燭，妻咿喔喔呀喔的又大哭起來。）

賈　這好極了！只要這樣就够了！等到他的畫統統賣完了，我再來通知你們！

　　（林妻哭着，弟則幫忙賈收集室內的圖畫，幕落。）

16　15　14　13　12　11　10　9　8　7　6　5　4　3　2　1

終身大事

胡適

戲中人物：

田太太　　　　　　　　　　　　　　　1

田先生　　　　　　　　　　　　　　　2

田亞梅女士　　　　　　　　　　　　　3

算命先生（瞎子）　　　　　　　　　　4

田宅的女僕李媽　　　　　　　　　　　5

布景：

田宅的會客室。右邊有門，通大門。左邊有門，通飯廳。背面有一張沙發　　6

椅。兩旁有兩張靠椅。中央一張小圓桌子，桌上有花瓶。桌邊有兩張坐椅。左邊　　7

榻。兩旁有兩張靠椅。中央一張小圓桌子，桌上有花瓶。桌邊有兩張坐椅。左邊　　8

靠壁有一張小寫字檯。　　　　　　　　　　　　　　　　　　　　　　　　　　9

牆上掛的是中國字畫，夾着兩塊西洋荷蘭派的風景畫。這種中西合璧的陳　　10

　　　　　　　　　　　　　　　　　　　　　　　　　　　　　　　　　　　11

設，很可表示這家人半新半舊的風氣。

開幕時，幕慢慢的上去，臺下的人還可聽見臺上算命先生彈的絃子將完的聲音。田太太坐在一張靠椅上。算命先生坐在桌邊椅子上。

田太太　你說的話，我不大聽得懂。你看這門親事可對得嗎？

算命先生　田太太，我是據命直言的。我們算命的，都是據命直言。你知道——

田太太　據命直言是怎樣呢？

算命先生　這門親事是做不得的。要是你家這位姑娘嫁了這男人，將來一定沒有好結果。

田太太　為什麼呢？

算命先生　你知道，我不過是據命直言。這男命是寅年亥日生的，女命是巳年申時生的，正合着命書上說的「蛇配虎，男尅女。豬配猴，不到頭。」這是合婚最忌的八字。屬蛇和屬虎的已是相尅的了。再加上亥日申時，豬猴相尅，這是兩重大忌的命。這兩口兒要成了夫婦，一定不能團圓到老。仔細看起來，男命強得多，是一個夫尅妻之命，應該女人早年短命。田太太，我不過據命直言，你不要見怪。

田太太　不怪，不怪。我是最喜歡人直說的。你這話一定不會錯。昨天觀音娘娘也是這

16　15　14　13　12　11　10　9　8　7　6　5　4　3　2　1

樣說。

算命先生　哦！觀音菩薩也這樣說嗎？

田太太　是的，觀音娘娘籤詩上說——讓我尋出來念給你聽。（走到寫字檯邊，翻開抽屜，拿出了一條黃紙，念道）這是七十八籤，下下。籤詩說，「夫妻前生定，因緣莫強求。逆天終有禍，婚姻不到頭。」

算命先生　「婚姻不到頭」，這句詩，和我剛才說的一個字都不錯。

田太太　觀音娘娘的話，自然不會錯的。不過這件事，是我家姑娘的終身大事。我們做爺娘的，總得二十四分小心的辦去。所以我昨兒求了籤詩，總還有點不放心。今天請你先生來看看這兩個八字裏可有什麼合得攏的地方。

算命先生　沒有，沒有。

田太太　娘娘的籤詩，只有幾句，不容易懂得。如今你算起命來，又合籤詩一樣，這個自然不用再說了。（取錢付算命先生）難爲你，這是你對八字的錢。

算命先生　（伸手接錢）不用得，不用得。多謝，多謝。想不到觀音娘娘的籤詩居然和我的話一樣！（立起身來）

田太太　（喊道）李媽！（李媽從左邊門進來）你領他出去。（李媽領算命先生從右邊門出去）

16　15　14　13　12　11　10　9　8　7　6　5　4　3　2　1

田太太　（把桌上的紅紙柬帖收起，摺好了，放在寫字檯的抽屜裏。又把黃紙籤詩也放進去。口裏說道）可惜！可惜這兩口兒竟配不成！　　　　　　　　　　　1

田亞梅女士　（從右邊門進來。她是一個二十三四歲的女子，穿着出門的大衣，臉上現出有心事的神氣。進門後，一面脫下大衣，一面說道）媽，你怎麼又算起命來了？我在門口碰着一個算命的走出去，你忘了爸爸不准算命的進門嗎？　　　　　　　2　3　4

田太太　我的孩子，就只這一次，我下次再不幹了。　　　　　　　　　　　　　　　　　5　6

田女　但是你答應了爸爸以後不再算命了。　　　　　　　　　　　　　　　　　　　　7

田太太　我知道，我知道，但是這一回我不能不請教算命的。我叫他來，把你和陳先生的八字排排看。　　　　　　　　　　　　　　　　　　　　　　　　　　　　8　9

田女　哦！哦！　　　　　　　　　　　　　　　　　　　　　　　　　　　　　　10

田太太　你要知道，這是你的終身大事，我又只生了你一個女兒，我不能糊裏糊塗的讓你嫁一個合不來的人。　　　　　　　　　　　　　　　　　　　　　　　11　12

田女　誰說我們合不來？我們是多年的朋友，一定很合得來。　　　　　　　　　　　13

田太太　一定合不來，算命的說你們合不來。　　　　　　　　　　　　　　　　　14

田女　他懂得什麼？　　　　　　　　　　　　　　　　　　　　　　　　　　　15

田太太　不單是算命的這樣說，觀音菩薩也這樣說。　　　　　　　　　　　　　　16

田女　什麼？你還去問過觀音菩薩嗎？爸爸知道了更要說話了。

田太太　我知道你爸爸一定同我反對。無論我做什麼事，他總同我反對，但是你想我們老年人怎樣敢決斷你們的婚姻大事。我們無論怎樣小心，保不住沒有錯。但是菩薩總不會騙人。況且菩薩說的話，和算命的說的，竟會一樣，這就更可相信了。（立起來，走到寫字檯邊，翻開抽屜）你自己看菩薩的籤詩。

田女　我不要看！我不要看！

田太太　（不得已把抽屜蓋了）我的孩子，你不要這樣固執。那位陳先生我是很喜歡他的，我看他是一個很可靠的人。你在東洋認得他好幾年了，你說你很知道他的為人。但是你年紀還輕，又沒有閱歷，你的眼力也許會錯的。就是我們活了五六十歲的人，也還不敢相信自己眼力。因為我不敢相信自己，所以我去問觀音菩薩，又去問算命的。菩薩說對不得，算命也說對不得，這還會錯嗎？算命的說，你們八字正是命書最忌的八字，叫做什麼「豬配猴，不到頭」，因為你是巳年申時生的，他是——

田女　你不要說了！媽，我不要聽這些話。（雙手遮着臉帶着哭聲）我不愛聽這些話！我知道爸爸不會同你一樣主意。他一定不會。

田太太　我不管他打什麼主意。我的女兒嫁人，總得我肯。（走到他女兒身邊，用手巾

替她揩眼淚）不要掉眼淚。我走開去，讓你仔細想想。我們都是替你打算，總

想你好。我去看午飯好了沒有，你爸爸就要回來了。不要哭了，好孩子。（田

太太從飯廳的門進去了）

田女　（揩着眼淚，擡起頭來，看見李媽從外面進來。她用手招呼她走近些，低聲說）

李媽，我要你幫我的忙。我媽不准我嫁陳先生——

李媽　可惜，可惜！陳先生是一個很懂禮的君子人。今兒早晨，我在路上碰着他，他還

點頭招呼我咧。

田女　是的，他看見你帶了算命先生來家，他怕我們的事有什麼變卦，所以他立刻打電

話，到學堂去告訴我。我回來時，他在他的汽車裏，遠遠的跟在後面。這時候恐

怕他還在這條街的口子上等候我的信息。你去告訴他，說我媽不許我們結婚。但

是爸爸就回來了，他自然會幫我們，你叫他把汽車開到後面街上去等我的回信。

你就去罷。（李媽轉身將出去）回來！（李媽轉身回來）你告訴他——你叫他——

你叫他不要着急。（李媽微笑出去）

走到寫字檯邊，翻開抽屜，偷看抽屜裏的東西。伸出手錶看道）爸爸應該回來

了，快十二點了。

（田先生約摸五十歲的樣子，從外面進來）

16　15　14　13　12　11　10　9　8　7　6　5　4　3　2　1

田女　（忙把抽屜蓋了，站起來接她父親）爸爸你回來了！媽說……媽有要緊的話同你商量——有很要緊的話。

田先生　什麼要緊話？你先告訴我。

田女　媽會告訴你的。（走到飯廳邊，喊道）媽！媽！爸爸回來了。

田先生　不知道你們又弄什麼鬼了。（坐在一張椅子上，田太太從飯廳那邊過來）亞梅說你有要緊話——很要緊的話，要同我商量。

田太太　是的，很要緊的話。（坐在左邊椅子上）我說的是陳家這門親事。

田先生　不錯，我這幾天心裏也在盤算這件事。

田太太　很好，我們都該盤算這件事了。這是亞梅的終身大事，我一想起這件事如何重大，我就發愁，連飯都吃不下了，覺也睡不着了。那位陳先生，我們雖然見過好幾次了，我心裏總有點不放心。從前人家看女婿，總不過偷看一面就完了。現在我們見面越多了，我們的責任，更不容易擔了。他家是很有錢的，但是有錢人家的子弟總是壞的多，好的少。他是一個外國留學生，但是許多留學生回來不久就把他們原配的妻子休了。

田先生　你講了這一大篇，究竟是什麼主意？

田太太　我的主意是，我們替女兒辦這件大事，不能相信自己的主意。我就不敢相信我

　　自己，所以我昨兒到了觀音菴去問菩薩。

田先生　什麼？你不是答應我不再去燒香拜佛了嗎？

田太太　我是為了女兒的事去的。

田先生　哼！哼！算了罷。你說罷。

田太太　我去菴裏求了一籤。籤詩上說，這門親事是做不得的。我把籤詩給你看（要去開抽屜）

田先生　呸！呸！我不要看。我不相信這些東西！你說這是女兒的終身大事，你不敢相信自己，難道那泥塑木雕的菩薩就可相信嗎？

田女　（高興起來）我說，爸爸是不相信這些事的。（走近他父親身邊）謝謝你。我們應該相信自己的主意，可不是嗎？

田太太　不單是菩薩這樣說。

田先生　哦！還有誰呢？

田太太　我求了籤詩，心裏還不很放心，總還有點疑惑。所以我叫人去請城裏頂有名的算命先生張瞎子，來排八字。

田先生　哼！哼！你又忘記你答應我的話了。

田太太　我也知道。但是為了女兒的大事，心裏疑惑不定，沒有主張，不得不去找他決

16　15　14　13　12　11　10　9　8　7　6　5　4　3　2　1

田先生　誰叫你先去找菩薩惹起這點疑惑來呢？你先就不該去問菩薩——你該先來問

我。

田太太　罪過，罪過，阿彌陀佛——那算命的說的話，同菩薩說的一個樣兒。這不是一

椿奇事嗎？

田先生　算了罷！算了罷！不要再胡說八道了。你有眼睛，自己不肯用，反去請教那沒

有眼睛的瞎子，這不是笑話嗎？

田女　爸爸，你這話一點也不錯。我早就知道，你是贊助我們的。

田太太　（怒向他女兒）虧你說得出，「贊助我們的」，誰是「你們」？「你們」是

誰？你也不害羞！（用手巾蒙面哭了）你們一齊通同起來反對我！我女兒終身

大事，我做娘的管不得嗎？

田先生　正因為這是女兒終身大事，所以我們做父母的，應該格外小心，格外慎重。什

麼泥菩薩哪，什麼算命合婚哪，都是騙人的，不可相信。亞梅，你說是不是？

田女　正是，正是。我早知道你決不會相信這些東西。

田先生　現在不許再講那些迷信的話了。泥菩薩，瞎算命，一齊丟去！我們要正正經經

的討論這件事。（對田太太）不要哭了，（對田女士）你也坐下。（田女在沙

發上坐下，下決斷。

（發楊上坐下）

田先生　　亞梅，我不願意你同那姓陳的結婚。

田女　　（驚慌）爸爸，你是同我開玩笑，還是當眞？

田先生　　當眞。這門親事一定做不得的。我說這話，心裏很難過，但是我不能不說。

田女　　你莫非看出他有什麼不好的地方？

田先生　　沒有。我很喜歡他。揀女壻揀中了他，再好也沒有了，因此我心裏更不好過。

田女　　（摸不着頭腦）你又相信菩薩和算命？

田先生　　決不，決不！

田太太與田女　　（同時問）那麼究竟爲了什麼呢？

田先生　　好孩子，你出洋長久了，竟把中國的風俗規矩全都忘了。你連祖宗定下的祠規都不記得了。

田女　　我同陳家結婚，犯了那一條祠規？

田先生　　我拿給你看。（站起來從飯廳邊進去）

田太太　　我眞意想不到。阿彌陀佛，這樣也好，只要他不肯許就是了。

田女　　（低頭細想，忽然擡頭顯出決心的神氣）我知道怎麼辦了。

田先生　　（捧着一大部族譜進來）你瞧，這是我們的族譜。（翻開書頁，亂堆在桌上）

田先生　你瞧，我們田家兩千五百年的祖宗，可有一個姓田的和姓陳的結親？

田女　爲什麼姓田的不能和姓陳的結婚呢？

田先生　因爲中國的風俗不准同姓的結婚。

田女　我們並不同姓。他家姓陳，我家姓田。

田先生　我們是同姓的。中國古時的人，把陳字和田字讀成一樣的音。我們的姓有時寫作田字，有時寫作陳字，其實是一樣的。你小時候不是讀過論語嗎？

田女　讀過的，不大記得了。

田先生　論語上有個陳成子，旁的書上都寫作田成子，便是這個道理。兩千五百年前，姓陳的和姓田的只是一家。後來年代久了，那寫做田字的便認定姓田，寫作陳字的便認定姓陳，外面看起來，好像是兩姓，其實是一家。所以兩姓祠堂裏都不準通婚。

田女　難道二千年前同姓的男女也不能通婚嗎？

田先生　不能。

田女　爸爸，你是明白道理的人，一定不認這種沒有道理的祠規。

田先生　我不認牠也無用。社會承認牠，那般老先生們承認牠。你叫我怎麼樣呢？還不單是姓田的和姓陳的呢。我們衙門裏有一位高先生告訴我，說他們那邊姓高的

祖上本是元朝末年明朝初年陳友諒的孫子，後來改姓高。他們因六百年前姓陳，所以不同姓陳的結親；又因爲二千五百年前姓陳的本又姓田，所以，又不同姓田的結親。

田女　這更沒有道理了！

田先生　管他有理無理，這是祠堂裏的規矩，我們犯了祠規就要革出祠堂。前幾十年有家姓田的，在南邊做生意，就把一個女兒嫁給姓陳的。後來那女兒死了，陳家祠堂的族長不准她進祠堂。他家花了多少錢，捐到祠堂裏做罰歇，還把「田」字中那一直拉長了，上下都出了頭，改成了「申」字，才許他進祠堂。

田女　那是很容易的事，我情願把我當中一直也拉長了改作「申」字。

田先生　說得很容易的事。你情願我不情願咧！我不肯爲了你的事，連累了我受那班老先生的笑罵。

田女　（氣得哭了）但是我們並不同姓！

田先生　我們族譜上說是同姓，那般老先生們也都說是同姓。我已經問過許多老先生，他們都是這樣說。你要知道，我們做爹娘的，辦女兒終身大事，雖然不該聽泥菩薩的瞎算命的話，但是那般老先生們的話是不能不聽的。

田女　（作哀告的樣子）爸爸！——

16　15　14　13　12　11　10　9　8　7　6　5　4　3　2　1

田先生　你聽我說完了。還有一層難處。要是你這位姓陳的朋友是沒有錢的，到也罷　1

了；不幸他又是很有錢的人家，我要把你嫁了他，那班老先生們必定說我貪圖　2

他有錢，所以連祖宗都不顧，就把女兒賣給他了。　3

田女　（絕望了）爸爸！你一生要打破迷信的風俗，到底還打不破迷信的祠規，這是我　4

做夢也想不到的。　5

田先生　你惱我嗎？這也難怪。你心裏自然總有點不快活，這種氣頭上的話，我決不怪　6

你——決不怪你。　7

李媽　（從左邊門出來）午飯擺好了。　8

田先生　來，來，來。我們吃了飯再談罷。我肚裏餓得很了。（先走進飯廳去）　9

田太太　（走近她女兒）不要哭了。你要自己明白，我們都是爲你好。忍住，我們吃飯　10

去。　11

田女　我不要吃飯。　12

田太太　不要這樣固執。我先去，你定一定心就來。我們等你咧。（也進飯廳去了。李　13

媽把門隨手關上，自己站着不動）　14

田女　（擡起頭來看見李媽）陳先生還在汽車上等着嗎？　15

李媽　是的。這是他給你的信，用鉛筆寫的。（摸出一張紙遞與田女）　16

田女　（讀信）「此事只關係我們兩人，與別人無關，你該自己決斷。」（重讀末句）

　　「你該自己決斷！」是的，我該自己決斷！（對李媽說）你進去告訴我爸爸和

　　媽，叫他們先吃飯，不用等我。我要停一會再吃。（李媽點頭自進去。田女士站

　　起來，穿上大衣，在寫字檯上匆匆寫了一張字條，壓在桌上花瓶底下。她回頭一

　　望，匆匆從右邊門出去了。畧停一會）

田太太　（戲台裏的聲音）亞梅，你快來吃飯，菜要冰冷了。（門裏出來）你那裏去了？

　　亞梅。

田太太　（戲台裏）隨她罷。她生了氣了，讓她平平氣就會好了。（門裏出來）她出去

田先生　（門裏出來）你那裏去了？

　　了？

田太太　她穿好了大衣出去了。怕是回學堂去了。

田先生　（看見花瓶底下的字條）這是什麼字條？（念道）「這是孩兒終身大事，孩兒

　　應該自己決斷。孩兒現在坐了陳先生的汽車去了。暫時告辭了。」（田太太聽

　　了，身子往後一仰，坐在靠椅上。田先生衝向右邊的門，到了門邊，又回頭一

　　望，眼睜睜的顯出遲疑不決的神氣。幕下來）

14　13　12　11　10　9　8　7　6　5　4　3　2　1

回家以後

歐陽予倩

登場人名：

紐約大學生陸治平　　　　　　　1

其妻吳自芳　　　　　　　　　　2

其父陸期昌　　　　　　　　　　3

其祖母顧氏　　　　　　　　　　4

其岳父吳有述　　　　　　　　　5

其再婚妻劉瑪利　　　　　　　　6

長工老陳　　　　　　　　　　　7

女僕張媽　　　　　　　　　　　8

村農王三及其他　　　　　　　　9

村婦四五人　　　　　　　　　　10

小孩數人　　　　　　　　　　　11

　　　　　　　　　　　　　　　12

地點：湖南鄉間

時候：秋季

佈景：一所鄉紳人家的儉樸的平房。當中大門。屋後有樹；山右邊是通村外的大道；左邊是些豆棚瓜架。門外打麥場上放着幾個曬衣叉，竹竿上曬着幾件外國衣服。地下有兩張板凳。張媽從門內上場。

張媽　太陽下山了，少奶奶！

自芳　（上場）讓我來收，你去伺候老太太去。她是耳朵不大聽見，回頭又說叫你不應。（顧氏在房內連叫張媽）

張媽　衣裳收起來罷？

自芳　甚麼？（內應）

張媽　衣裳收起來罷？

自芳　（上場）讓我來收，你去伺候老太太去。她是耳朵不大聽見，回頭又說叫你不應。（顧氏在房內連叫張媽）

張媽　唯唯！

自芳　是不是，叫你了。（張媽笑着下。自芳一面收拾衣服，一面自言自語）這個口袋脫了線，讓我慢慢兒替他縫一縫罷。（她仔細看那衣服的製法，無意中在口袋的

1　2　3　4　5　6　7　8　9　10　11　12　13　14

夾層裏抽出兩片乾荷花瓣，很爲奇怪）唔！外國裁縫，還拿花瓣襯在衣服裏呢．

唔！怎麼還寫着字？（念道）「永遠的愛情，維持我們永遠的生活．」（又念那

一片）「無量的愛情，產生我們偉大的事業．」（她呆了半晌，再將花瓣念一遍，

自言自語道）人家都說治平另外又跟人家結了婚，先總當是謠言，誰知被我找出

證據來了。原來海誓山盟都寫在這花瓣上．（正在低頭吟思，老陳自門內出來．）

老陳　菜是都預備好了，那個白切肉還是您來切罷．

自芳　你放在那裏就是了．（精神不屬的樣子，把花瓣收起．）

老陳　老爺少爺還沒回呢．時候還早，我去看看水車去．不知道修好了沒有？（一面說

着，一面向右邊走去．）

自芳　你去罷．（治平自外面回來．）

治平　自芳，你在這裏幹甚麼？

自芳　替你曬這些寶貝衣裳呢．

治平　謝謝，不敢當．

自芳　你真客氣，美國人對女人是比中國人對女人客氣些．

治平　男女本來平等，自然應當客氣一點兒．

自芳　客氣就是平等嗎？

16　15　14　13　12　11　10　9　8　7　6　5　4　3　2　1

治平　那不盡然。可是禮節也是要的，中國不是也說「相敬如賓」麼？

自芳　怪不得你在家裏是作客一樣。

自芳　人生本來到處作客。（拿出煙來抽。）

治平　咳！美國城裏做的衣裳拿到中國的鄉下來曬。

自芳　我不能永遠在美國，我總要離開回來的；並且我回家以後，覺得一草一木，都是非常自然。像我們這種鄉村，只要沒有西洋人物質的勢力來壓迫我們，我們真是別有天地，極其快樂。那些繁華都市的罪惡一樣也看不見，貧富的階級，相差也不遠。許多天然的物產同簡單的生活，只要有明白人來加以指導，讓他自自然然一天一天進化，多麼好呢？

治平　你怎麼會知道鄉下的風味？

自芳　我怎麼不知道！我方纔走過我小時候念書的關帝廟，又到了外祖母家裏，他們後山的竹子上，還有我刻的字呢。從前小時候的情景宛在目前，不知不覺使我愛鄉的心油然而生。

治平　但可惜在鄉下沒人安慰你。

自芳　你不是我的好伴侶麼？

治平　在你學問沒有成就的時候，或者我可以作你的伴侶。如今你在美國大學得了學

治平　位，我就够不上了。

治平　你够不上，誰够得上？

自芳　自然有人够得上。

治平　我以爲祇有一個人够得上。

自芳　誰？

治平　吳自芳（說得很柔媚。）

自芳　（微微冷笑）我又沒有到過外國，又不會音樂跳舞。

治平　何必要會？

自芳　我又不會會。

治平　我又不會交際。

自芳　交際有什麽道理？

治平　學問是專爲擺架子的嗎？

自芳　我又沒有學問可以拿來擺架子。

治平　（畧緩以壯語勢）我又不會拿花瓣來寫情書。

自芳　（變色）這是甚麽話？

治平　何必這樣兒着急呢？我不過是說說好頑兒罷了。

自芳　你一定聽見人家甚麽不相干的話了。

16　15　14　13　12　11　10　9　8　7　6　5　4　3　2　1

自芳　別怪旁人。這也是你自己不小心露了破綻。（對衣服說）謝謝你傳給我這樁有趣的新聞呀。我今日纔知道「永久的愛情，纔能够維持永久的生活」呢。

治平　自芳，你這是甚麼意思？

自芳　你也用不着假裝不知道。前年一走，就聽說你在外國另外跟人家結了婚。不是前天公公還問你，你說沒有嗎？

治平　本來……。

自芳　當時總說是謠言。有許多幸災樂禍的人，因為你平日自命是進德會的發起人，所以聽見你有這種事，便格外加油加醬的當笑話兒說。我呢，以為你是個正直有為的青年，以為你能够體貼老人家期望你的一片苦心；所以人家儘管說得有憑有據，我儘管替你辯論，並且拿我的良心來保證你决無其事。誰想我今天在你衣服的夾層裏頭，無意中看見你們在荷花瓣上寫的字，這纔知道你跟人家結婚是真的。（村農王三持電信數封並報紙上。）

王三　大少爺，少奶奶，這是城裏李先生專人送來的一包信，放在這裏罷。

治平　放在這裏就是，謝謝你。

王三　不容客氣，我去了。

自芳　喝杯茶去。

王三　我去了，謝謝少奶奶，我去了。（走去）

自芳　這裏頭一定有你的那個人寫給你的信。

治平　沒有的話，不要管她。

自芳　不要管她？

治平　我很對不起你。

自芳　見着我就說不要管她，她不是一樣的人麼？何況是你心愛的人！要說對得起我對不起我，與我毫不相干。只望你仔細想想將來怎麼樣？

治平　我也有我的苦衷。

自芳　因為她實在可愛，怎麼能够不愛呢？

治平　你又來了。不是這樣說。我到了美國非常寂寞，你又在萬里之外；忽然有人來安慰我，我似乎不能辜負人家的好意。所以……。

自芳　所以就以身許之。

治平　所以就彼此成了朋友。

自芳　所以就拿結婚來報答朋友。朋友是非結婚不能報答的啊！

治平　由你說去罷。

自芳　她姓甚麼？

治平　姓劉。

自芳　不錯，人家也說是姓劉。我還知道她的名字叫瑪利（取出花瓣），這兒寫着呢！

治平　還給你吧，別讓你心痛。

自芳　你不留着作憑據嗎？

治平　憑據在心裏。——你眞心愛她？

自芳　我跟她是朋友之愛。如今男女社交本是公開的。

治平　要不拿海誓山盟寫在花瓣上就算不得朋友之愛了。……你對她也曾說起過我麼？

自芳　我常常說起你。她也很想跟你作個朋友。

治平　中國的學堂裏爲甚麼不設言語一科？美國的學堂是很注重這一科的。

自芳　我並不說假話。

治平　眞假與我不相干。

自芳　你恨我麼？

治平　先問你愛她嗎？

自芳　你又來了！

治平　我看你不見得愛她，我也不願意恨你。你要是愛她，你就不會騙她。我要是恨

自芳　你，除非我從來就不愛你。

治平　你不愛我嗎？可是我越聽你的話，越覺得你可愛。

自芳　快別這樣說，我眞是害怕死了。

治平　我眞是愛你。

自芳　那我就沒有生路了。

治平　你說的話我眞不懂。

自芳　你的話我又何嘗明白。

治平　我在外頭就算是偶然有些不大安當的地方，也不過一時候的事情。於我的良心毫不相干。並且多經一次閱歷，跟你的愛情就增加一分，你或者不肯信，你始終總要明白的。

自芳　據你這樣說，胡鬧的事情越多，情分纔能好。結婚的次數越多，良心纔能堅固。這纔知道那些荒唐的人，都是在那裏求閱歷。

治平　自芳，你……太……，似乎太……。

自芳　你想說「似乎太過」，是麼？我們鄉下人從來不懂得甚麼叫愛情。這不過是熱鬧場中的一句俏皮話。我不幸認識幾行字，就在書裏報裏見着多少女人都死在這種俏皮話底下。唉！你可以算了罷。……唷！只顧說着話，就誤了多少光陰，花還沒澆，菜還沒切，酒還沒去倒呢。你的衣裳我給你照樣放在你自己的皮包裏去

治平　（取衣）。別就誤你看信要緊。（一面說，一面拿起衣服，微微冷笑。自芳走進門去，治平望着她說。）

　　　　　（看信。老陳上。）

老陳　大少爺，你這下不再出去了罷？老爺眞擔不少的心。謠言又多，說是您討了洋婆子不回來了。少奶奶可眞是度量寬宏……。（治平急拿話止住他。）

治平　老陳你剛從那裏來？

老陳　去修水車來。鄕下人車水是眞苦啊，要有機器就好了。你們外國什麼都是機器。

治平　大少爺，我聽見說，人的身子也是一個機器，可以拆開來修修的……又說外國人還能拿人的肚腸子剖出來，洗好了再放進去，是眞的嗎？

老陳　是眞的。

治平　啊，那眞奇怪！頂好心也可修理，那就更妙了。我們中國人有心病的也實在多，黑心的也眞不少。最好請個外國機器匠來修修。

老陳　哈哈！要把人修成機器，那就糟了。

治平　不過就怕外國人不肯眞把中國人的心修好，反而要修壞了。聽說外國人不抽鴉片

氣，坐下拿起信來，自言自語）這封是她的。唉！眞不該回家……，可是……。

（望着自芳進門，呆立無語，深吸了一口

隨便你怎樣說罷，我也是無可如何。

治平：煙，儘逼着中國人抽，我想這也是弄壞人心的手段。我們的心還是別讓人家修，還是我們自己修修罷。

老陳：你說的話倒也有些道理。

治平：聽說你們到外國去念書，一定有洋婆子來灌迷魂湯，喝了就叫你忘掉本國，真的嗎？

老陳：那兒有這樣的話，胡說八道。你去罷，我還有事呢。（轉身）

治平：真是那兒的話，我們又不是三歲小孩兒，難道曾被人暗算了去，這不是笑話嗎！……（一面走，一面回頭望治平笑說道）十幾歲時候，翻壇打廟，不知多淘氣，如今倒也看了世界回來了（說着走進屋裏去）。她要萬一趕了來，怎麼辦呢？……

兩孩子：（忽然聽見山歌之聲，一男一女唱着上。）郎去耕田妻在家，煮好飯來煎好茶。朋友夫妻都一樣，他幫着我來我幫着她。鄉下的夫妻講恩愛，城裏的夫妻講衣裳。衣裳舊了換新的，恩情越舊越久長。（兩個小孩子看着治平，互相耳語，指指笑笑。治平忽擡頭瞧他們一眼，他們就

大笑跑了。治平正在凝思，張媽上，端着一個茶盤，盤裏一隻碗，正要送與治

平。治平的祖母顧氏，從裏面大聲叫住張媽。一面叫着，走了出來。）

顧氏　張媽，張媽，慢着，慢着！

張媽　不是送給少爺吃的嗎？（一面說，一面作手勢。）

顧氏　慢着，慢着，少奶奶，少奶奶！（自芳上。）

自芳　作甚麼？奶奶，奶奶。

（顧氏招招手，又對治平指指，望着盤裏的蓮子羹，作手勢，意思叫自芳送去與

治平。自芳會意。雖然笑着應允，不免總露一些兒勉強之態。張媽卻在一旁着

口笑。自芳將盤端近治平。）

治平　（不安的樣子，把幾封信插在衣袋內。自芳看見這種情形，又是好笑，

又是不屑。）

自芳　謝謝你！（治平回頭看見祖母，祖母微笑。

治平　在這兒想些甚麼？有甚麼為難的事？這是祖母親手剝好的蓮子羹給你吃的。

自芳　膽兒放大些……快謝謝祖母罷（扶祖母）。（治平回頭看見祖母，祖母微笑。

這時張媽搬張椅子請顧氏坐下。）

怎麼您老人家還親手作蓮子羹給我吃。真是，我倒沒有孝順您老人家的……

治平　（顧氏正像沒大聽見，只管自己說話。）

16　15　14　13　12　11　10　9　8　7　6　5　4　3　2　1

顧氏　糖够不够？

治平　够了。（點頭）

顧氏　聽說你回來了，從荷葉發生就等起，原說是等你回來看荷花。

自芳　（從旁插一句）荷花瓣上好寫字。

　　　（治平大吃一驚。）

顧氏　甚麼？（自芳搖搖頭，笑着走去。）

自芳　沒有甚麼。（下）

顧氏　誰知道蓮蓬都快老了，好容易你纔回來。咳！你們在外頭甚麼好吃東西沒吃過，誰還吃這些鄉下東西？這不過是老人家一點意思罷了。

治平　外頭也沒有甚麼好吃的。

張媽　少爺，您總要大聲些兒，老太太聽不見。（治平正想再說。）

顧氏　老陳，雞鴨都關好了沒有？……

老陳　（內面答應）一隻也不少，關好了。

張媽　關好了。

顧氏　前回那隻黃鼠狼只怕不敢再來了。少爺愛吃雞蛋，別讓牠咬了我們的母雞。

張媽　少爺會說外國話，黃鼠狼一定不敢來。

16　15　14　13　12　11　10　9　8　7　6　5　4　3　2　1

治平　胡說八道。

張媽　牠怕少爺拿洋槍打牠。

顧氏　治平你倒喜歡吃這個。

治平　（大聲）鄉下的東西樣樣都新鮮，所以好吃。在大都會就吃不着這樣新鮮的蓮子。

顧氏　你要吃大頭菜，鄉下也有新鮮的。

治平　（治平笑。）

　　　不是，我說是大都會，是說城裏樣樣沒有鄉下新鮮。

顧氏　是啊，城裏的菜，都是鄉下去的，時候隔久了，就不甜了。可是菜不甜事小，沒有熱鬧看事大。我也幾時要到你們上海去看看，就只怕人家看着鄉下老太婆像妖怪；回頭我沒有看着熱鬧，反被人家當熱鬧看了去。哈哈哈！（都笑。治平吃完。）你够了嗎？

治平　我不吃了，真好吃。

顧氏　可惜還老了一些兒。嫩的時候還要好吃，嫩蓮子心也是甜的；等你來，蓮子老了，蓮子的心也苦了。（笑）咳！你出去的時候，我那裏捨得，可是男子志在四方，誰能够老留在家裏。一直等到接了信，知道你平安到了外國，這纔放心。好容易

又聽見說你要回來了，我又擔心你在路上。有一晚我作一個夢，夢見你坐在一隻 1

大海船上，穿一身光燦燦的衣裳，有很多的洋婆子圍着你。忽然船壞了，許多的 2

人都掉在海裏，大家叫救命。彷彿我在一個高坡上看見，急得甚麼似的。我忽然 3

朝下一跳，好像身上長了翅膀一般，立刻從波浪裏頭將你抱了起來，放在沙灘 4

上，看看你已經沒氣了。我只好仰天大哭，你被我哭轉過來。正在歡喜的時候，忽 5

然來了一個西洋婆子，跟蹤兒似的，一隻手伸在你的膀子裏，拉着你就走了。 6

我又恨又氣，正要追上去，有人拍拍我的肩膀說：「這不是你的世界，他也不是 7

你的孫兒。」說着，對準我頭上一棒打來，我就醒了，還是睡在牀上。（又將聲 8

治平 音變低說）因爲那時有人造過你的謠言，所以我這些胡思亂想的夢，也就沒有說 9

給自芳聽。（顧氏囉囉索索只管說，治平因爲別有心思，糊裏糊塗亂答着。） 10

日有所思，夜有所夢。——吃飽了就睡，也要作夢的。（其父期昌，其岳丈吳有 11

期昌 述，同自外面走來，正好將話叉開。） 12

有述 請，請，（大家相見）媽，出來了。 13

有述 姻伯母。 14

顧氏 親家來了。 15

有述 您老人家出來坐坐，天氣眞好，今天你精神也覺得格外的好。（顧氏聽不大明 16

顧氏　　白，期昌轉述一遍。治平前去與有述周旋。張媽搬出幾張椅子。）

顧氏　　親家，如今孫子也成了人，一門團聚，甚麼不歡喜？我人也真好了，肝氣也平了，
　　　　飯也比從前吃得下些。……您請坐。張媽去倒茶。叫聲少奶奶。（張媽下。）

有述　　您請坐。

顧氏　　親家請坐。

有述　　親家喝茶。

　　　　（張媽倒茶上。自芳來接着茶，先叫聲有述，送杯茶；次顧氏，次期昌。顧氏讓
　　　　親家喝茶。）

有述　　您請喝茶。

顧氏　　怎樣少爺還沒有茶呢？張媽！

張媽　　唷！少倒了一杯，再去倒罷（笑着下。）

治平　　我不要喝茶。（自芳搬出一張小桌子放在當中。）

顧氏　　親家！從前人家都造謠言，治平不回來了，如今還不是回來了麼？人不回到家
　　　　裏，回到那裏去？造謠言的人真可恨，還說他討了洋婆子呢。（大家都笑。自芳
　　　　望着治平。治平也隨便笑笑。）

期昌　　現在年輕的人，本來糟糕的也很多。

有述　　世道人心，到了今日，本有不可測的地方。總得有幾個中流砥柱的人才挽回頹風

16　15　14　13　12　11　10　9　8　7　6　5　4　3　2　1

張媽　　才好。治平將來一定是大有可爲的（張媽上。）

顧氏　　陳司務請少奶奶去弄菜。

顧氏　　少奶奶，你去罷。老陳弄的菜吃不得，治平歡喜吃新鮮雞蛋，你好好兒弄雞蛋給他嘗嘗。（自芳笑着答應下去，顧氏又趕着說。）他是歡喜外國派半生半熟的，不要太老了。

有述　　老太太眞會疼孫子，眞會疼孫子。

顧氏　　可憐他祖父去世太早，好容易將他父親守大，全靠着作針線跟人家洗衣裳拿一家撐持起來。一直等到期昌拔了貢以後又在甚麽法政學堂裏畢了業，我們家裏方始過着一些好的日子。

期昌　　那時候學堂還很少，我們在法政學堂畢業出來，好像很新奇似的；而且馬上就有事情做。（有述點頭）

顧氏　　期昌娶了親就生了治平。可憐我那媳婦不久就去世了，沒有見着治平的成就。

有述　　（大家嘆息）我五十歲的時候，期昌的朋友們，定要跟我豎甚麽牌樓……

顧氏　　那時節我還來請過您的示呢。

有述　　我那時候說牌樓眞沒有意思。只要大家能够替治平想法子弄個官費讀書，就比甚麽都好。總算大家幫忙，如了我的心願。一個人在世界上空名聲有甚麽意思，只

16 15 14 13 12 11 10 9 8 7 6 5 4 3 2 1

要作事於心無愧就是了。可憐我是一點本事都沒有，又沒有甚麼依傍；現在是老 1

了，格外沒有用了。我也不想享兒孫的福；只要兒孫能夠在世界上作一個有用的 2

人，便死也閉得口眼了。 3

有述　兒孫有用，還不就是長輩的福氣嗎！ 4

治平　治平我是真疼他。老實說，我待他父親是比待他嚴得多。有了獨子最怕溺愛不 5

顧氏　明，所以格外要嚴些。 6

期昌　治平他們念書比我們從前容易多了，我們從前想念書，可是沒有書，連借都借不 7

着。 8

有述　如今念書可也真不容易。學費之貴…… 9

治平　並且書又很貴，隨便買一本，幾十塊錢不算甚麼。 10

有述　從此以後，只怕寒士就沒有受高等教育的機會了。 11

期昌　前回看見報上有一個學生向他父親要錢，父親說他用得太大，問他除學費外還有 12

甚麼費用。他說還要女朋友的交際費，說是沒有女朋友，念書念不進去，哈哈！ 13

　　　（有述笑，治平也隨便笑笑。） 14

有述　那就讓他早討親好了。 15

期昌　本來是討過的。 16

有述　那就格外的該死了。（又笑笑，又嘆嘆氣。自芳上。）　1

自芳　飯好了，擺在後面小廳上呢，還是就在這裏？　2

有述　就在這裏罷。　3

期昌　何不就在這空地上？……姻伯母呢？　4

自芳　媽就吃飯麼？　5

期昌　我到裏頭去，他們坐罷……親家坐。　6

有述　您老人家別客氣，外面風也大。　7

顧氏　您請坐，我現在是真經不起風浪了。（顧氏指點着自芳，又叫張媽幫着擺好桌椅。）　8

期昌　請坐罷。　9

顧氏　治平，你多敬你丈人幾杯。親家，您別客氣，榮是您姑娘作的，一定合您的口味。　10

有述　這都是您教導得好。　11

顧氏　那兒的話？回頭吃完了飯，叫治平說些海外的新聞我們聽聽。我想明年是要拿房子收拾得好，請親家來喝喜酒呢。（大家一笑。顧氏進去，期昌有述治平入座。）　12

有述　治平斟酒，自芳上菜，大家請酒。（自芳下。）　13

顧氏　她老人家精神真好。　14

期昌　我們家裏多虧她老人家。要是沒有她老人家，就沒有我們這一家了。從前先君去　15

　　　　　　　　　　　　　　16　15　14　13　12　11　10　9　8　7　6　5　4　3　2　1

有述：世，外祖母接她老人家回去。她老人家說：「這還不是時候呢，等把兒子養大，陸家的門戶撐持起來，再回娘家。」咳！現在那裏還聽得着這種話。卻是她老人家也就真受了不少的辛苦。不過有了治平，總算是她老人家替陸家造就了一個為國出力的人才，也就心滿意足了。

期昌：治平呢，也不能馬上就說是人才，不過到底受過些家庭教育，比普通一班的青年總靠得住一點。

有述：那是自然……啊！好風……甚麼香？

治平：好像是桂花。

期昌：這都是你令媛種的。

有述：自芳的種花念書，是成了癖性。

自芳：還要酒罷？

有述：酒也夠了罷。

期昌：再去添上一壺。（自芳拿着酒壺斟完，進去。）

有述：今天暢快極了，可以暢飲。

治平：村酒也別有滋味。我生長在鄉下，始終還是歡喜鄉下的生活。所以回國以後，不知不覺的想回家；回家以後，就好像印證平生的夢境似的，把作小孩子時候的事

有述　情從新翻檢出來。又聽見祖母跟父親說起許多古話，越覺得中國的社會，有一種積累下來的精神。　1

治平　這是不錯的。　2

有述　早晨醒來，聞着花香，聽着鳥語，比車水馬龍的熱鬧，自然受用得多。就是鄉下人簡單樸實的生活，也比鈎心鬭角的競爭省些煩惱。不過我們爲世界潮流所壓迫，不能不向那絕大的漩渦當中去討生活罷了。（自芳送酒來。）　3　4　5　6

期昌　你這話頗爲沉痛中肯。　7

有述　只怕是從繁華地方回來偶覺得清靜簡單的有趣罷。　8

治平　不然，一個人總有愛惜故鄉之心。我們生長的地方是我們一身的故鄉。我們在十五二十時所受的教訓，就是我們心的故鄉。如今的人，一面捨不得故鄉，一面愛好他鄉，所以又是煩悶，又沒有主意，弄得莫明其妙爲止。可是無論他們的心遊到甚麼幻境，始終還是要回想到他們故鄉的景況。　9　10　11　12

有述　本來中學時代所受的教育，往往支配人一生的思想。有的時候受別種思想的壓迫，生出一種懷疑，便引起很大的苦痛；這種情形，往往影響到一個人的行爲上。　13　14　15

有述　思想的壓迫倒還好，只怕是外面的引誘。　16

期昌　外面的引誘倒還好，只怕自己跟自己搗亂。

有述　不錯不錯，剛才你說的那個沒有女朋友不能念書的人，那就眞是自己跟自己搗亂。治平，對不對？（治平不安，無可掩飾，只有發笑。）

治平　哈哈，哈哈！

有述　話也說得不少了，酒也喝得够了，最好吃飯罷。

期昌　再喝兩杯，等素榮來再吃飯。

有述　榮太多了……治平這次回家，暫且不出去罷。

治平　我本想在家多住些時，只是方才有個外國朋友從漢口寄來一封信，說是要同我組織一個貿易公司。他因爲急於要回國去，不能在漢口久候。只專等我去拿事情商量安了，他就趕着上海的定期船回國。我恐怕……今天晚上就要動身呢。（期昌，有述大驚。）

期昌　今天晚上？怎麼一直沒有說起！

有述　遲一兩天，許還不甚要緊罷。你怎麼來得及呢？

治平　恐怕遲了就要誤人家的船期。

期昌　從前你跟他沒有約會嗎？

治平　唔……有是有過……。

有述　貿易公司不是一椿小事，倒會忽然發生，而又迫不及待呢。

治平　我是怕錯過這機會（自芳送菜上。）

自芳　爹，這是自己家裏的泡菜，您嘗嘗看。

期昌　少奶，治平說他今天晚上就要動身到漢口去。（自芳頗覺驚異，馬上又鎮定。）

有述　他說有個外國朋友約他去開公司，今晚就走，只怕來不及罷。你也不知道嗎？

自芳　我……不知道，我只知道他有個已經組織好了的公司，恐怕有點新交涉，他要去
……（治平搶說。）

治平　那是你弄錯了。

有述期昌　甚麼公司？

治平　自芳完全弄錯了，因為我曾經提起過別人的公司。

自芳　公司總是越多開越好，不過自己多煩點兒神能了。——爹，您多喝杯酒罷，飯還
要等一會兒，老陳下米下遲了。（翩然下。）

期昌　既是一定有要緊的事呢，自然應當去。今天晚上坐轎子還好趕火車。祖母面前，
我來替你稟明，你大約事情商量安了，就好回來。

治平　只要不擔重大的責任，總回來得快的。（有述將治平喚過一邊。）

有述　治平，來，我跟你說兩句話……男兒志在四方，本不能長留你在家裏；只是你母

　　　親老人家去世你很早，祖母愛你撫養你的深情，你總不能忘記。能彀早回最好，多　1

在家裏住住，安慰安慰老人家的暮年。住兩三個月，總不至於就誤你甚麼大事。　2

這話他老人家是不想對你講，恐怕拿家事絆住了你的前程。要知道你的前程無　3

限，祖母的年紀可是大了，猶如太陽已經靠了山，那流戀骨肉的餘光還照在你的　4

身上。你祖母是個慷慨義烈的女丈夫，她維持陸氏一家，決不想圖子孫的報答，　5

可是作子孫的卻也不能置大恩於不顧。　6

治平　那個自然，我應當拿我將來的事業報答祖母。　7

有述　顯親揚名自然是一件事，承歡色笑也是不可缺的。（漸說漸走回席，自芳上。）　8

自芳　爹，這是甜菜。　9

有述　我勸治平這回去了，總要早些回來。（坐下。）　10

期昌　那邊誰來了，不是王三嗎？……啊！還有人。（王三跑上。）　11

王三　唉，老爺，少爺，吳老爺！……少爺，我來報信的。　12

治平　啊，怎麼？　13

王三　坐着轎子，還有縣裏派的人送來的。他們來問路，在茶店裏喝茶，我所以先來報　14

個信。女洋人說的好像中國話，我怕聽不懂，沒敢多說。回頭說得好就好，說得　15

不好，就是一個耳刮子。　16

　　　　　　　　　　　　　　　　　　　　　　有個女洋人找你來了。

期昌　誰會來找你？

治平　想必是朋友來遊歷的。

期昌　來了，來了……洋姑娘洋太太，這裏呢。（劉瑪利上，後面跟的轎夫，用人，並

王三　一輩鄉下男女。期昌，有逃都站起來。自芳明明知道是治平的新妻，偷看治平的

治平　態度。治平不知所可。瑪利暫不發言。）

治平　吾愛，你怎麼會來？

瑪麗　我怎麼不會來？難道你還不許我來。

期昌　（問治平）這位女士是誰？

治平　這是劉女士。

自芳　這不是瑪利女士嗎？……這就是我公公，這就是我家嚴，治平就是外子。

瑪利　治平，你已經有妻子的嗎？

期昌　小兒娶親已經七八年了。女士，這是甚麼話？

瑪利　（指治平）你這敗類，……害人的賊。你說你沒有娶過親。你千方百計騙我。

治平　（老陳出來看着奇怪。）

治平　千方百計騙你，我實在沒有。

瑪利　止，……你我在美國，不過見幾次面，你就動手騙我。後來結了婚，問你的家

16　15　14　13　12　11　10　9　8　7　6　5　4　3　2　1

有述

期昌

自芳

事，你說跟腐敗的家庭早已脫離關係。一直等回到上海，才有我舊時的同學可憐我，來告訴我，說我上了你的當；說你娶我，并不是作妻，只是作妾。那時你已經回家來了，我也無從盤問。你回家時候，你說只到漢口經營煤礦公司，那時你還說出多少的不便，不許我跟你同走。誰知我以後才打聽到你是怕你父親到上海找你，所以急於回家敷衍你父親。我一連打了好幾個電報——差不多每天一個，試試你是否在漢口。誰知一個沒有回電，兩個沒有回電，三個四個還是沒有回電，我才決意自己來看你。我幸喜我哥哥跟這裏縣知事有些認識，寫了封信託他照應。你以爲能够一生一世藏着躲着嗎？你以爲我是軟弱無能，隨便讓人欺負的女子嗎？（盛怒，拉張椅子坐下，望着治平。期昌也盛怒。）

原來漢口的貿易公司就是這麼回事。（說着看治平，回過臉走，嘆氣。）

治平，你會作這種事嗎？這種事情也是你作的嗎？想不到你會敗壞我們的家風到這步田地，想不到你會敗壞你自己的人格到這步田地！家庭跟學校總算給了你一些教育，何以你會這樣兒不知自愛？（自芳微微低首，瑪利憤極而悲；大家長嘆無語。張媽此時溜出來何事。自芳趕向張媽說話。）

你跑出來幹甚麼？快去快去。跟老太太不要說起，別讓她知道。（張媽一面聽自芳說話，一面望着新來的客發怔。自芳跟她咬咬耳朵，推她走去。老陳看得心裏

1
2
3
4
5
6
7
8
9
10
11
12
13
14
15
16

治平　明白。）

老陳　唉，怎麼謊言變了眞事？少爺，你總要拿出主意來，別叫老爺着急才是。（他一面去趕那些看的人，一面讓轎夫等到後面去喝茶。轎夫等隨老陳繞到屋後去，那些鄉下人退了一退，仍然擠上。有述還想說話，治平已經開口。）

治平　求爸爸恕我。我並不是不知自愛，我今天拿我的事和盤託出，就當作我表示我的懺悔。我自從跟自芳結婚，我覺得她多少事莫明其妙，所以我跟她的愛情本來不甚濃厚。到了外國，看見歐美婦女那種活潑溫柔的情形，不禁非常羨慕，所以才有跟這位劉女士結合的事情。那時候恐怕不是歐風美雨浸潤過的劉女士還不能引起我的顧盼。我此番回家原想求父親跟岳父商量，要跟自芳離婚。（有述大驚，自芳亦不免愕然。期昌握拳長嘆。惟有瑪利女士抬起頭望望治平，似含無窮的柔

期昌　媚與哀怨，也用尖細的聲音，嘆了一口氣。）

治平　該死該死，該死到萬分！

瑪利　你回家以後怎麼樣？便怎麼樣？

治平　誰知我回家以後，……（瑪利急了。）

期昌　我回家以後又發現了自芳不少的好處——是新式女子所沒有的好處。

瑪利　我不許你再往下說！我不許你再往下說！

治平　（有氣沒力的）瑪利，你不許我懺悔嗎？我覺得一切事情都不過是一時候感情的變遷。

瑪利　感情這樣容易變遷，還成人嗎？

瑪利　感情要沒有變遷，那不成了麻木不仁了嗎？

治平　治平，你竟敢在我面前說這種不莊重無賴的話，真是豈有此理。我真想不到有你這樣不知廉恥的兒子！

期昌　老先生，您有多少遺產給治平！

瑪利　這是甚麼話？我那裏有甚麼遺產給治平。我所給治平的詩書禮義，都被他弄得破產了。

期昌　兒子過了二十一歲，就不歸父母管束。如今的年月，除非是父親有很多的遺產，才有資格管束兒女呢。目下您教訓治平已經遲了，只問怎樣解決今天的問題。空口說白話是沒有用的。

有述　這我可不能忍了！天底下那有這種事情。總而言之，男女的關係本是雙方的，既不能專怪治平引誘劉女士，也不能竟說劉女士單獨引誘治平。總而言之，世道人心，一天比一天壞，到了今日，真是青年男女墮落的大關鍵……

瑪利　你說誰墮落？

16　15　14　13　12　11　10　9　8　7　6　5　4　3　2　1

有述　聽我說完。就今天而論，劉女士怎麼能够那樣兒質問長輩，就算治平是朋友，期 1

昌　先生自然也在父執之列。劉女士似乎措詞失當。治平呢，方才的話，太覺狂妄 2

　　無稽，也不是對父親應該說的。至於自芳，是我的女兒，是治平的髮妻，應該… 3

有述　……（瑪利搶說。） 4

瑪利　老先生，你這是甚麼話？甚麼叫作引誘？甚麼叫措詞失當？這分明是侮辱人！你 5

　　應當知道公然侮辱是甚麼罪名？ 6

期昌　這些都不必辯論，只是當初女士跟治平結婚的時候爲甚麼不打聽打聽明白呢？ 7

有述　一生的大事能够那樣兒草率，隨隨便便就跟人家結婚嗎？治平有不對的地方，我 8

　　們自然責備治平。女士有不安的地方，我們可也不能贊同。總而言之，治平是有 9

　　婦之夫，女士大約也應當明白自己的地位。 10

瑪利　我也不願意跟你們這些半開化的人多說廢話，反正治平的名譽信用，將來的希 11

　　望，甚至於性命，都在我手裏。我決不能放過他。治平，你還裝腔嗎？ 12

治平　你要怎麼樣呢？ 13

瑪利　你說怎麼樣。 14

治平　（有述拉期昌一旁去說話） 15

治平　一夫一妻的制度本來是很好的。不過美國也有一種一夫多妻的宗教。法國現在爲 16

治平：人口問題，也正獎勵一夫多妻的制度。我千萬對不起你，只好慢慢兒再來贖罪。一切都因為愛你而起，我的心是始終沒變，你總可以原諒。并且你還可以慢慢兒瞧着我到底是不是一個薄倖的人。我決不主張一夫多妻的辦法，不過今天我想對你作一次例外的要求。自芳實在眞是一個很有思想的女子，我願你暫且把目下的事情攔一攔，先跟自芳作個朋友。好在我又不能够飛到那裏去，你們先把你們的人生觀交換的研究研究，然後再來處置我，好不好呢？（有述與期昌雖是在一旁，仍然聽着看着。）

瑪利：治平，你別弄錯了，我可沒有功夫跟你說廢話。（不理他）。

治平：（對自芳）自芳，你自己已經介紹過了。我縱然不足齒數，你們不妨見見。（說到此處看看期昌跟有述）爸爸跟丈人為兒女操勞得够了。

有述：我可沒有為兒女這樣操勞過。

治平：我的不孝，本來，除掉拿這一生來懺悔，不能補救於萬一；只是決不想拿兒女本身的事情再多叫老人家操心。難道我們就不能自己想個妥當的法子嗎！（說時，很莊重的樣子。）

瑪利：這毫不與我相干（說時帶一種輕侮而淡漠的微笑）。

自芳：治平。

16　15　14　13　12　11　10　9　8　7　6　5　4　3　2　1

瑪利

自芳　自芳，你進去。

有述　自芳，你進去。

自芳　爸爸，你放心罷。我要是避開，不怕怠慢了客麼？

治平，你不用再支吾了。如今只有兩個條件：一，你趕緊跟這鄉下的女子正式離婚；二，你以後一切的事情，要絕對受我的監督。你有本事你就殺了我，不然就絕對的服從我。你要想再弄一些兒狡獪，我能夠叫你一生所受的苦痛比自殺還要利害。趕快，趕快！五分鐘以後不許你再遲疑了。害人的賊，專門會把當給人上。

期昌　這……這是從那裏說起？

有述　這是中華民國所沒有的吧？（許多鄉下人都在那裏發着笑，作些怪相，老陳出來趕開他們。）

老陳　有甚麼好看？有甚麼意思？還不是那麼一回事。差不多的人家都有的。去啊，去啊！（衆人散去）少爺，你怎麼毫沒主意。今天馬馬糊糊混過，最好造一座東樓，一座西樓，請少奶奶跟洋太太搖彩票，誰頭彩就住東樓。……

治平　走開！

期昌　治平，你怎麼樣？

有述　唉！（自芳看着不得下臺，打定主意，很大方的走到劉女士面前。）

自芳　瑪利女士，我跟你雖然是初見，大家都是女人，總不妨表同情的。

有述　自芳，自芳。（以目示意，叫她不要說話。）

自芳　我願意爸爸許我說完幾句話。

瑪利　治平，怎麼樣？只有三分鐘了。

自芳　我求瑪利女士完全當我是不相干的局外人，聽我幾句最誠懇的話。（治平很怕她說出不妥的話，想止住她，又不敢。）我跟治平結婚以來，治平常不在家，他並沒有深知我，我也沒有甚多的機會可以深知他。我父親跟治平的老人家是好朋友，我嫁到這裏來，好比送我寄住在父親的朋友家裏一樣。

期昌　少奶奶，你這是甚麼意思？

自芳　我也不過是這樣想罷了。

有述　唉！

自芳　我常常想，結婚跟離婚，都不過是一種形式，我是從來沒有在這種形式裏求幸福。世界這樣大，難道沒有別一個境界能夠容得下我們。治平跟女士結婚的時候，他心裏本來沒有我，所以他對女士說他從來沒有娶過親。恐怕他哄騙女士，正是他愛女士最深的地方。治平因為愛女士才大胆娶女士，女士因為愛治平才放心嫁治平。我決不願拿我這局外人來作煞風景的事，更不願勉強算人家的妻子，

期昌　來看不起我自己。劉女士。你放心罷，你跟治平是夫妻。

少奶，這是甚麼話？那怎麼能夠？

自芳　自芳，你是甚麼意思？

有述　爹顧全女兒，女兒也不過顧全自己，顧全一家。我想劉女士決不能久在鄉下，治平，幾千里路結伴同行，可以溫習舊時的功課了。你的行李是很簡單的，我來替平在倉促之間也沒有辦法。求公公還是讓治平送劉女士回上海去。（對治平）治

期昌　你預備罷。（正想下去。）

少奶，慢着。我決不讓治平為這種事情離開家裏去。

有述　親家，我方才想自芳的話很有深意。我們已經是過時的人了；我看解鈴繫鈴，還是讓治平自己去了結罷。

期昌　唉！⋯⋯

瑪利　無論你們是手段也好，是誠意也好，只要治平能履行條件就完了。（張媽上。）

張媽　少奶奶請來罷，老太太說，好像外面很多人說話，問是誰呢。她老人家，說她全不聽見，有時好像全聽見。（指指瑪利）怎麼還沒去？

自芳　你別管，你去罷。我就來。（說着走了進去。）

治平　瑪利，你的條件我都明白了，我們有話⋯⋯你這兒來，我跟你說。

　　　　　　　　　　　　　　　　　　　　　　　　　　　　16　15　14　13　12　11　10　9　8　7　6　5　4　3　2　1

瑪利　（意欲引瑪利一旁去。）

瑪利　我們沒有甚麼祕密，有話公開說。

治平　Particularly to you.

瑪利　外國話我不懂。

治平　治平不必遲疑了。應當怎麼辦就怎麼辦罷。別儘自己跟自己搗亂了。

有逃　啊，我真沒見過這種卑劣無賴的男人。我真受不了這種煙霧漫天的光景。我再要

站在這裏，一定被野人吃了去。真想不到像我這樣受過高等教育的人會受這種侮

辱。喂，轎夫！（對治平）我不怕你跑了天上去。你再能出頭就算你……轎夫！

老陳　（她氣得上氣不接下氣。老陳上。）

格外大聲。

瑪利　洋太太，你叫轎夫，我就去。你輕一點兒；老太太聽見，不得了。（急下。瑪利

治平　治平，你要放明白，你休想再轉灣了，你休想我再饒恕你，你休想能逃出羅網。

你記住，這是你欺我，騙我，侮辱我，逼迫我，使我不得不用我最後的手段！

（加重）我最後的手段，你不要後悔！（轎夫上。）走！

治平　瑪利。

瑪利　走了，走了，走了，我一生拚給你了。你不要後悔！（下）

　　　　　　　　　　　　　　　　　　　　　　16 15 14 13 12 11 10 9 8 7 6 5 4 3 2 1

有述　（這還不是野人嗎？（他憤極，望着瑪利的背影。期昌手足顫動，連話都說不出來。）

期昌　我，我一家都完了！我辛辛苦苦撐持的一家完了，完了！

治平　爸爸放心，那是萬不會的。

期昌　你說不會，你說不會！

治平　劉瑪利縱然利害，也不致破壞我一生。

期昌　不要人家來破壞，你自己已經破壞你自己了。劉女士不知自愛，不去說她，家裏還有你的妻子呢。你怎麼對得起她？又怎麼對得起丈人？我自此還有甚麼面目見人！祖母倘若知道，又怎麼樣？你自己是不用說了。劉女士就算好說話，社會上也未見得能夠寬容你，你自己的良心更不能夠放過你。你只顧一時的糊鬧，弄得多少人爲你受盡苦處，你於心何忍？我也不忍往下多說，只看你怎麼恢復你本來的面目。（說到這裏，非常沉痛。自芳上，提一個皮包放在門旁。）

治平　爸爸，我並沒有忘卻我的本來面目。總而言之，我可以算是懦弱糊塗的了。

期昌　分胡鬧，或者不完全是胡鬧。論起來，前後的事情都有些關連，或者有幾分胡鬧，我並沒有忘卻我的本來面目。

自芳　恐怕不止懦弱糊塗罷？劉女士去了嗎？

有述　去了，祖母沒有問起麼？

自芳　劉女士大聲說話的時候，祖母就聽見了，問甚麼事，我支吾開了。祖母本來還想出來坐坐。剛才吹了點兒風，頭有點不舒服，我就服侍她老人家睡下了。她老人家還替治平打算這樣，打算那樣。咳，她老人家愛治平，眞是無所不至。（對治平）行李收拾好了。

有述　（行李收拾好了。）

期昌　少奶奶，你太好了，治平辜負你，你還替他打算。你的意思是要叫他慚愧，他那裏知道。可是我決不讓他辜負你。

有述　停妻再娶，本來是法律所禁，但是我們決不願拿這個來責備治平；只望治平憑他自己的良心來處置這件事情。

治平　我也決不辜負自芳。

自芳　說不到辜負的話，還是你自己檢點檢點自己的事情，別讓人說你一回家就使大家不安。至於我，在家裏承父母十分鍾愛，來到這裏，祖母舅姑待我比自己子女還好。我本來歡喜鄉下，我愛種花，愛養鷁，愛讀書，自然有好多世界，在我這方寸之中。我本無求於人，又何求於你？況且我最佩服祖母的爲人，她老人家辛苦一生好容易使兒孫都能成立。我不要說是孫子媳婦，就算是鄰居，我也願意常常來安慰她老人家。如今她老人家所望的只有治平，目下這件事，

治平　一定教她老人家傷心。我不忍，我以爲還得想法子娛她老人家的晚年才是。請治平不要再提自芳的事，自芳自然有自芳的主見。……時候不早了，你也自己決定罷。去罷。（期昌有述同聲長嘆。）

有述　自芳，難道你不可憐嗎？

自芳　你不能這樣說，她是個可憐的女子。

自芳　她已經跟我決裂了，還有甚麼說的？

自芳　天底下只有失望的人跟乞憐於人的人是最不幸，是最可憐。我本不求人憐，也就不受人憐。本來沒有求人的地方，也就沒有失望的苦楚。治平沒有回家是怎麼樣？他回家以後又是怎麼樣？豆棚瓜架不適於金迷紙醉的人物，錦繡繁華也不適於鄉村的女子。……唷，這麼半天，荣也冷了，應當去熱熱了。

期昌有述　用不着熱了。

自芳　不費事的（端着荣就走。）

治平　自芳，自芳。……（自芳回頭。）

自芳　你的話不用說，我都知道。（下）

治平　想不到這幾年，自芳的學問思想進步得這樣快。

期昌　想不到這幾年，你的道德品行退步得這樣快。

有述　天下事想不到的太多了。（苦笑）

治平　如今也無法可想，只好暫且去把那邊的事情辦妥後再回家來。

期昌　恐怕再帶些些不幸回來。

治平　過去的事不能消滅，未來的事也難於限量。咳，男女的關係好像南極探險，空留得後人許多談助。今天的事是我一生的大轉機，從今以後，我認準我努力的路徑了。社會決不棄我，天還是要給我們幸福。爸爸，我暫且一去。（期昌垂頭無話）

有述　大人，還求您格外看重自芳。

　　　　自芳，她倒還頗知自重，不用你煩心，只願你此番得着個徹底覺悟的機會。（治平對有述期昌鞠躬，回頭提一提皮包，又放下，叫老陳。老陳上。）

老陳　作甚麼？

治平　你替我搬着這個皮包到前面鎮上去，雇乘轎子趕火車。

老陳　老爺答應麼？（望着期昌。）

治平　老爺答應了。

老陳　剛回來，又要去，老太太怎麼捨得？看起來迷魂湯還是利害。（一面說着，背着皮包下。治平看看錶，想進去看自芳。自芳正端着飯菜從裏面走出，治平前去叫一聲，自芳畧爲停步，欲不理他，治平湊近前說。）

　　　　　　　　　　　　　　　　　　16　15　14　13　12　11　10　9　8　7　6　5　4　3　2　1

治平　祖母醒了沒有？　　　　　　　　　　　　　　　　　　　　　　1

自芳　還沒有呢。　　　　　　　　　　　　　　　　　　　　　　　　2

治平　我不敢驚動。回頭他老人家醒了，請你說我有要事往城裏去了，兩三天就回來。　3

自芳　家裏的事不要你煩心。（治平對期昌有述鞠躬，又向自芳示意。自芳將飯慢慢擺　4
　　　在桌上。治平無精打采的走下。期昌目送之，憤極而悲。有述握住自芳的手叫。）　5

有述　自芳。（自芳輕輕答應。此時又聽見前頭那兩個小孩唱山歌之聲。自芳低頭不　6
　　　語。）　　　　　　　　　　　　　　　　　　　　　　　　　　　　　　　　　7

　　　　　　　　　　　　　　　　　——幕——　　　　　　　　　　　　　　　　　　8

第二部

詩　歌

教我如何不想她

劉　復

天上飄着些微雲，
地上吹着些微風。
啊！
微風吹動了我頭髮，
教我如何不想她？

月光戀愛着海洋，
海洋戀愛着月光。
啊！
這般蜜也似的銀夜，
教我如何不想她？

　　10　9　8　7　6　　5　4　3　2　1

水面落花慢慢流，

水底魚兒慢慢游。

啊！

燕子你說些什麼話？

教我如何不想她？

枯樹在冷風裏搖。

野火在暮色中燒。

啊！

西天還有些兒殘霞

教我如何不想她？

一九二○，九，四，倫敦。

11　10　9　8　7　6　　5　4　3　2　1

一笑

胡適

十幾年前， 1

一個人對我笑了一笑。 2

我當時不懂得什麼， 3

只覺得他笑的很好。 4

那個人不知後來怎樣了， 5

只是他那一笑還在： 6

我不但忘不了他， 7

還覺得他越久越可愛。 8

我借他做了許多情詩，　　　　　　　　　　　　　　　1

我替他想出種種境地；　　　　　　　　　　　　　　　2

有的人讀了傷心，　　　　　　　　　　　　　　　　　3

有的人讀了歡喜。　　　　　　　　　　　　　　　　　4

歡喜也罷，傷心也罷，　　　　　　　　　　　　　　　5

其實只是那一笑。　　　　　　　　　　　　　　　　　6

我至今還不曾尋着那笑的人，　　　　　　　　　　　　7

但我很感謝他笑的眞好。　　　　　　　　　　　　　　8

詩的宣言

郭沫若

你看，我是這樣的眞率，　　　　1

我是一點也沒有什麼修飾。　　　2

我愛的是那些工人和農人，　　　3

他們赤着腳，裸着身體。　　　　4

我也赤着腳，裸着身體。　　　　5

我仇視那富有的階級：　　　　　6

他們美，他們愛美，　　　　　　7

他們的一身：綾羅，香水，寶石。　8

我要如暴風一樣怒吼。

我希望我總有一天，

我的氣魄沒有以前雄厚。

這是我纔恢復不久，

我還要經過鍛鍊一番。

我雖然還軟弱了一點，

我的階級是屬於無產；

我的詩，這便是我的宣言，

8　　7　　6　　5　　　　4　　3　　2　　1

雪花的快樂

徐志摩

假如我是一朵雪花，

翩翩的在半空裏瀟灑，

我一定認清我的方向——

飛颺，飛颺，飛颺，——

這地面上有我的方向。

不去那冷寞的幽谷，

不去那淒清的山麓，

也不上荒街去惆悵——

飛颺，飛颺，飛颺，——

你看，我有我的方向！

10　9　8　7　6　　　5　4　3　2　1

在半空裏娟娟的飛舞，

認明了那清幽的住處，

等着她來花園裏探望——

飛颺，飛颺，飛颺，——

啊，她身上有硃砂梅的清香！

那時我憑藉我的身輕，

盈盈的，沾住了她的衣襟，

貼近她柔波似的心胸——

消溶，消溶，消溶，——

溶入了她柔波似的心胸！

　　　　　10　9　8　7　6　　5　4　3　2　1

聞一多先生的書桌

聞一多

忽然一切的靜物都講話了，
忽然間書桌上怨聲騰沸：
墨盒呻吟道：「我渴得要死！」　1
字典喊雨水漬濕了他的背；　2

毛筆講火柴燒禿了他的鬚，　5
鋼筆說煙灰閉塞了他的嘴，　6
信箋忙叫道彎痛了他的腰；　7
鉛筆抱怨牙刷壓了他的腿；　8

字典喊雨水漬濕了他的背；　3
墨盒呻吟道：　4

香爐咕嘍着：「這些野蠻的書

早晚定規要把你擠倒了！」　　　　　　　　　　　　　　1

大鋼錶嘆息快睡銹了骨頭；　　　　　　　　　　　　　　2

「風來了！風來了！」稿紙都叫了；　　　　　　　　　　3

筆洗說他分明是盛水的，　　　　　　　　　　　　　　　4

怎麼吃得慣臭辣的雪茄灰；　　　　　　　　　　　　　　5

桌子怨一年洗不上兩回澡，　　　　　　　　　　　　　　6

墨水壺說：「我兩天給你洗一回·」　　　　　　　　　　7

　　　　　　　　　　　　　　　　　　　　　　　　　　8

「什麼主人？誰是我們的主人？」

一切的靜物都同聲罵道：

「生活若果是這般的狼狽，

倒還不如沒有生活的好！」

主人敲着煙斗，迷迷地笑：

「一切的衆生應該各安其位。

我何曾有意的糟塌你們，

秩序不在我的能力之內。」

　　　　　　　　8　7　6　5　　　4　3　2　1

繁　星

謝冰心

繁星閃爍着——
深藍的太空，
何曾聽得見他們對語？
沈默中，
微光裏，
他們深深的互相頌讚了。

嫩綠的芽兒，
和青年說：
「發展你自己！」
淡白的花兒，
和青年說：
「貢獻你自己！」

12　11　10　　9　8　7　　6　5　4　　3　2　1

深紅的果兒，
和青年說：
「犧牲你自己！」

成功的花，
人們只驚慕她現時的明艷！
然而當初她的芽兒，
浸透了奮鬥的淚泉，
灑遍了犧牲的血雨。

大海呵，
那一顆星沒有光？
那一朵花沒有香？
那一次我的思潮裏
沒有你波濤的清響？

13　12　11　10　9　　8　7　6　5　4　　3　2　1

我是一條小河

馮　至

我是一條小河，　　　　　　　　　　　1

我無心由你的身邊繞過——　　　　　　2

你無心把你彩霞般的影兒　　　　　　　3

投入了我輕輕的柔波。　　　　　　　　4

我流過一座森林——　　　　　　　　　5

柔波便蕩蕩地　　　　　　　　　　　　6

把那些碧翠的葉影兒　　　　　　　　　7

裁剪成你的裙裳。　　　　　　　　　　8

我流過一座花叢——

柔波便粼粼地

把那些悽豔的花影兒

編織成你的花冠。

無奈呀，我終於流入了，

流入那無情的大海——

海上的風又厲，浪又狂，

吹折了花冠，擊碎了裙裳！

我也隨了海潮漂漾，

漂漾到無邊的地方——

你那彩霞般的影兒

竟也同幻散了的彩霞一樣！

一
九
二
五

13　12　11　10　9　　　8　7　6　5　　　4　3　2　1

過橋

李廣田

記得嗎，那時是兩個孩子，　　　　　　　　1

大雨後，在河邊的草地上遊戲？　　　　　2

赤腳踢碎了滿地的珍珠露；　　　　　　　3

聽我們的歌，天上的行雲也暫駐。　　　4

「蟬蛛在東，」你唱天上的虹，　　　　5

望着虹，笑，又啞住了歌聲。　　　　　7

你問我：「那虹像不像一座橋，　　　　6

那麼長，那麼彎，跨過了雲天，一挖？」　　8

「是的，」我回答：「那就是天上的橋，

到天國的樂園去，只那一條道。

等幾時，我們都不復是孩子，

要領你去天國，同過那彩橋。」

三十年後，我們又從這兒過，

沒有雲，沒有虹，秋的原野。

你又問：「面前那河橋像不像虹？」

不回答，默默地攜手從橋上過。

　　　　　　　　8　7　6　5　　　　4　3　2　1

望

下之琳

1　小時候我總愛望夏日的晴空，

2　把它當作是一幅自然的地圖：

3　藍的一片是大洋，白雲一朵朵——

4　大的是洲，小的是島嶼在海中；

5　大陸上顏色深的是山嶺山叢，

6　許多孔隙裂縫是冷落的江湖，

7　還有港灣像在望風帆的歸途，

8　等它們報告發現新土的成功。

望

如今，正像是老話的滄海桑田，

滿懷的花草換得了一把荒煙；

就是此刻我也得像一隻迷羊，

帶着一身灰沙，幸虧還有蔚藍，

還有彷彿的雲峯浮在縹渺間，

倒可以擡頭望望這一個仙鄉。

6　5　4　3　2　1

預　言

何其芳

這一個心跳的日子終於來臨。　　　　　　　　　　1

你夜的歎息似的漸近的足音，　　　　　　　　　　2

我聽得清，不是林葉和夜風私語，　　　　　　　　3

麋鹿馳過苔徑的細碎的蹄聲。　　　　　　　　　　4

告訴我，用你銀鈴的歌聲告訴我，　　　　　　　　5

你是不是預言中的年輕的神？　　　　　　　　　　6

你一定來自溫郁的南方，　　　　　　　　　　　　7

告訴我那兒的月色，那兒的日光，　　　　　　　　8

告訴我春風是怎樣吹開百花，　　　　　　　　　　9

燕子是怎樣癡戀着綠楊，　　　　　　　　　　　　10

我將合眼睡在你如夢的歌聲裏，　　　　　　　　　11

那溫馨我似乎記得又似乎遺忘。　　　　　　　　　12

請停下，停下你長途的奔波，

進來，這兒有虎皮的褥你坐，

讓我燒起每一秋天拾來的落葉，

聽我低低唱起我自己的歌，

那歌聲將火光樣沉鬱又高揚，

火光樣將落葉的一生訴說。

不要前行，前面是無邊的森林，

古老的樹現着野獸身上的斑文，

半生半死的籐蟒蛇樣交纏着，

密葉裏漏不下一顆星，

你將怯怯地不敢放下第二步，

當你聽見了第一步空寥的回聲。

12　11　10　9　8　7　　6　5　4　3　2　1

一定要走嗎？等我和你同行，

我的足知道每條平安的路徑，

我將不停地唱着忘倦的歌，

再給你，再給你手的溫存，

當夜的濃黑遮斷了我們，

你可不轉眼地望着我的眼睛。

我激動的歌聲你竟不聽，

你的足竟不爲我的顫抖暫停，

像靜穆的微風飄過這黃昏裏，

消失了，消失了你驕傲的足音……

啊！你終於如預言所說的無語而來

無語而去了嗎？年輕的神？

一九三一年秋

13　12　11　10　9　8　7　　6　5　4　3　2　1

太陽

從遠古的墓塋
從黑暗的年代
從人類死亡之流的那邊
震驚沉睡的山脈
若火輪飛旋於沙丘之上
太陽向我滾來……
牠以難遮掩的光芒
使生命呼吸
使高樹繁枝向牠舞蹈
使河流帶着狂歌奔向牠去

艾青

10　9　8　7　　6　5　4　3　2　1